文學研究叢書・臺灣文學叢刊

傳說的高砂族

秋澤烏川　著
許　俊　雅　編

鳳氣至純平
許　倍　榕　譯
崔　　麈

感謝國立臺灣師範大學
「原住民族永續發展的優質教育」
經費補助

自序

　　一八九五年，臺灣割讓日本，初期殖民地政府面臨種種統治上的困境，除了臺灣人的武力反抗之外，尚有「理蕃事業」的千頭萬緒。為了掌握山地資源，臺灣總督府自一九〇九年「臺灣舊慣調查會」成立「蕃族科」後，全面展開蕃族調查，並從一九一三年起陸續出版各種調查報告。一批批具有人類學專業背景的學術探險家如鳥居龍藏、伊能嘉矩、森丑之助先後來臺，在官方或學術團體經費挹注下，調查規模與採錄資料日趨成長，深入瞭解臺灣原住民現況，以及其歷史文化語言，累積了為數可觀的各族傳說。他們多數具備學術研究素養，採錄作業多合乎現今田野調查的程序，註記採錄的時間、族群部落名稱、故事來源（講述者），採取盡量不改動故事原文，以字母標記原音，正文添加對語彙、物品或習俗的註解，以及採錄期間觀察到的現象及個人心得，這種種做法不僅增加了故事原貌的可信度、真實性，也讓人類學、民俗學和語言學、文學等不同專業領域者，從中挖掘想要的資訊，延伸出更多的研究及創作。

　　臺灣原住民族因為沒有文字，以口傳吟誦的方式代代訴說著他們的故事，口傳文學在原住民族部落生活裡既是他們真實生活的一部分，關於儀式、習俗的學習傳承、價值觀的影響都在生活的過程逐漸完成。口傳文學所說之事多為族群的起源、分布及生活經驗、禁忌，以及射日、洪水、人類始祖來源等宇宙奧秘的種種解讀與部落曾發生過的事件，雖然有許多故事充滿奇幻色彩，但卻是理解其風土民情，

便於管理之道。所以當時駐守在原住民族聚居區域的警察，除以理蕃為首要任務，管理轄區內的原住民外，同時也蒐集整理相關原住民的事物，彙報給臺灣總督府。其中所記錄的原住民神話傳說，有些僅是故事梗概而非整體，或撰寫者依照自己的意思，將故事隨意刪減修改；或執筆者只做小範圍的實地探訪；或整理編纂既有的故事文本，沒有附註採錄時間、地點、口述者身分等相關資料。本書所錄傳說是一九二四年秋澤烏川所書寫。秋澤烏川曾擔任臺南地方法院書記，先受臺灣日日新報社之託，在該報上發表二十多回，後重新精選資料，撰有《臺灣日日新報》的〈生蕃の傳說と童話〉，《臺灣警察協會雜誌》的〈傳說の高砂族〉等。另編著有《臺灣匪誌》、《臺灣名流卓上一夕話》、《新舊對照管轄便覽》等書。其中《臺灣匪誌》，詳錄了臺人武裝抗日事跡，包括北埔事件、林杞埔事件、羅福星事件、土庫事件、六甲事件、西來庵事件，雖是以殖民統治者之立場撰述，仍具有重要的史料價值。這些神話故事在日本《臺灣警察協會雜誌》上發表，因此，隱含的讀者群比這裡的預期更為具體。

　　本書五回不依據族群名稱，而以內容性質為分類項目，再列出符合項目的各族故事，因此全書紀錄了二十一則故事，篇目是：〈久遠神代的故事〉、〈取得火種的故事〉、〈搗蛋神的故事〉、〈女護島的故事〉、〈征伐太陽的故事〉、〈日、月、星的故事〉、〈變成雷電的故事〉、〈舉天王鳥的故事〉、〈風、雨、雪的故事〉、〈開始狩首的故事〉、〈開始分家的故事〉、〈獨木舟的故事〉、〈預言者的故事〉、〈二神變成鶴的故事〉、〈少女入月的故事〉、〈少女變成鷲的故事〉、〈女人森林的故事〉、〈穿山甲與猴子的故事〉、〈開始刺青的故事〉、〈無人島的故事〉、〈祭祀夜晚的故事〉，展現每個族群獨特的風土民情，以及口傳故事在各族之間分布的情形。

　　收錄的故事，包括射日、族群始祖、猴子與穿山甲、父母化身為

鶴、女兒國故事、少女變成鷲的故事等等，有時不專屬某一族獨有，這是在流傳過程中常有的現象。未知的世界，經常是想像力的來源，當人類無法解釋地震、暴風雨、酷熱天候時，就會編說故事解釋這些現象，這反映了先人看世界的方法及內心的想望。如射日對遠古的民族而言，太陽的光線和熾熱所造成的災害，是難以避免且無法抵擋的，於是產生了許多征伐太陽的神話，利用自己經歷的生活經驗，表現出杜絕太陽肆虐的原始思維。秋澤烏川解釋〈征伐太陽的故事〉就說：「住在寒帶和溫帶地區的人因為害怕寒冷，所以極為尊敬熾盛有熱力的太陽，將其視為主神，把照亮黑夜的月亮視為從神。而住在熱帶及亞熱帶地區的人則相反，厭惡酷暑，崇敬夜間皎潔月光的清朗，將其視為主神，而太陽是從神。至於極端酷暑之地，甚至還會敵視太陽。」臺灣原住民族如布農族、泰雅族、阿美族都有類似射日的傳說。〈風、雨、雪的故事〉中，風、雨、雪各自誇耀自己的力量，較量結果是雪略高一籌，說明了住在高山不知害怕風雨的高砂族，是多麼害怕寒冷，這也與臺灣四季如夏的炎熱天候有關。另〈舉天王鳥的故事〉亦雷同，鳥兒 Tatachiyu 清亮、純淨、遼朗的聲音，使天地為之震動，天便迅速地往上層升去，使人類脫離熾烈炎熱之苦，得以在地面上安穩生活，Tatachiyu 也成為萬鳥之王。

　　〈取得火種的故事〉以平時盡受其他野獸侮辱的羌仔，憑著昂揚的勇敢志氣，克服巨浪的吞噬而取得火種，以此故事傳達那平常遭人責罵卻能隱忍自重的人，一旦有事發生，反而能夠發揮很大的力量。〈開始狩首的故事〉裡 Nibunu 神為了去除惡人而降下大洪水，人類無法覓食，狗、猴被殺後，首級被插在竹竿上玩，族人瘋狂跳起馘首舞，使得神明減退大水，丘陵和原野重現眼前，而之後改獵狩其他部落人的首級。〈開始刺青的故事〉講刺青由來，母子成為夫婦，而非姊弟或兄妹成為夫妻。這個母子版的人類祖先到下一則的〈無人島的

故事〉成為兄妹結為夫妻，子女又相互結為夫妻，分灶各自成家，終於形成一個部落。留在島上的是高砂族的祖先，離開島的則是臺灣人的祖先。阿美族流傳的傳說則是夫妻之神遺留下的男女二神 Sura 與 Nakao 結為夫婦，並未說明兄妹或姊弟關係。關於人類祖先的起始，流傳著情節相似的故事，有時也是對習俗由來的想像與解釋，比如賽夏族的黥面即仿泰雅族，以避免被誤殺。在神話傳說裡就描述姐姐怕被弟弟認出，因此以黑炭塗其臉，後來成為黥面由來。

〈失去女兒化身為鶴的神〉，海神強行娶走美麗的女兒神，巨濤摧毀了快樂的家庭，傷心的父母神最後化身為鶴飛向天際。秋澤烏川〈二神變成鶴的故事〉故事與此相近，最後都強調了雌雄成雙成對的畫面。這些故事的主角與人類相同，有著欲望、猜忌、情愛、誘惑、嫉妒、自私、貪婪性情以及憐憫、慈愛、堅毅、奮鬥種種情懷，這些故事是想望的投射，同時也具有教育的意義。

這些神話傳說也表現出各族的生活習俗，如阿美族神話故事——女人島傳說：〈女護島的故事〉，表現出阿美族「母系親屬制度」觀念，同時含括了阿美族男主外、女主內的分工模式。有時也反映時局，在日美為敵狀態下，衍生了對美國的嘲諷，如〈久遠神代的故事〉敘述了臺灣人類祖先從木石二質的老樹誕生，形成兩個部落，人數多、威力大的部落到平地，成為臺灣人祖先；有刺青、人數少的留在山上，成為高砂族的蕃人祖先。秋澤最後以之嘲諷美國的「人種歧視」，人與人之間是有差別區分的。再者，也有充滿幻想與娛樂效果的巨人故事，〈搗蛋神的故事〉敘述變化自如的搗蛋神 Idotsuku 惡作劇的故事，傳達原住民趣味無窮的生活。在作者不可思議的話語裡，也呈現當時對高砂族的形容是慓悍無比的。

略而歸納之，這五個系列，大抵第一個系列包括傳說，其中大部分是關於更古老的神話事件，物種起源，刀耕火種形式的農業開始、

女人國故事等。第二組故事中，許多自然現象都得到了科學的解釋，包括天體和天氣條件，日、月、星、雷電的由來等。第三組主要涉及部落習俗的起源，如獵頭和家族／部落分離。第四組中，女性的嫉妒佔據了中心舞臺，繼母虐待繼女的故事，最後一組人類始祖的起源及穿山甲與猴子的故事、祭祀故事。以上有許多主題是普遍的，如大洪水、始祖起源、征服太陽等，世界上許多文化在他們的神話中都有自己的版本，在語言上或圖像上記錄他們自己的生活故事。臺灣原住民族故事或者是生活環境相鄰，故事交互流傳影響下，在各族可見情節相似之故事。前述被繼母虐待的孩子變成鳥或升入月亮的故事、巨人或鳥將天空往上推的傳說、女人國對男人存敵意的現象、火燒動物彼此相爭的情節等均是。

秋澤烏川所編撰的傳說故事不多添油加醋多予鋪敘，傾向較為簡略，有些甚至不如其他版本完整，但此書漢譯本乃是首次面市，希望讀者閱讀譯本時，能對原住民的神話及傳說產生興趣，了解原住民特有的文化、藝術、習俗、禁忌、歷史沿革與蕃社變遷。雖然時過境遷，對當代讀者而言，這些故事實用價值不再，但其文學的意涵卻歷久彌新，仍值得細加品讀。

最後，我要再度感謝三位譯者的辛勞，沒有他（她）們辛勤的付出，這本譯著不可能出版。他們是中譯者鳳氣至純平、許倍榕及英譯者崔麿。此外，本書插圖為陳映蹀、汪凱彬的佳作，使內容文圖並茂，更具閱讀樂趣。也有勞編輯廖宜家小姐的協助，以及臺師大文學院「原住民族永續發展的優質教育」計畫經費的支援，與萬卷樓出版社的支持。此書如果能夠幫助讀者認識理解臺灣原住民族文學，則編者譯者幸甚。

許俊雅

二○一八年九月二十日

目次

輯三

輯四

輯五

Translation

輯一

傳說的高砂族（一）

傳說，是民族性的反映，是非文字的歷史。我前幾年受臺灣日日新報社之託，在該報上發表拙稿二十多回。然而，因為是利用公務餘暇時間每日撰寫，因此相當駁雜，實在不好意思。這次重新在本誌執筆〈傳說的高砂族〉，希望盡可能精選資料，並留意記述內容。若有幸引起讀者的興趣，那將是筆者所企盼的。

久遠神代的故事

那是距今三千年的神代往昔，在中央山脈稱為 Bunohon（ブノホン）的地方，有棵頗巨大的無名老樹。那巨木的半面是木質，另一半面是石質，蒼鬱青葉亭亭覆蓋了天日，世界一直是黑暗的。

某個夏天的傍晚，這棵樹精化成神，在此孕生所有生物。從樹幹下部誕生的，一個是有四腳、身上覆蓋毛皮；另一個是頭上有瘤，其形狀宛如樹木，軀幹上有兩樹枝與兩樹根。接著在樹幹上部誕生的，一個是形狀細長，不會步行，總是匍匐；另一個不在地上，而是擁有在空中飛翔的翅膀。這些就是後世人稱之為獸類、人類、蛇類、鳥類的祖先。

無奈因為世界是黑暗的，因此儘管生於同一棵樹上，也無法互相交談，然而某日，在一個偶然的機會裡，所有生物聚集在同一個巖窟。這時候，後世成為萬物靈長的人類祖先，首先開口說道：

「各位，我們過去只飲風裏腹，但不知為何，我總覺得肚子餓到不行，各位難道沒有那樣的感覺嗎？」

於是，獸類祖先彷彿等待這一刻很久似地熱切附和：

「當然，我們如今已是若不吃點什麼的話，根本沒辦法維持生命了。你看，我的肚子已經餓扁了。」

第三個加入話題的，是陰森的蛇類祖先：

「沒錯，不管什麼都好，我想趕快大口吞食填飽肚子。喂，你也跟我一樣吧！」

被這麼一問而最後出現的，是可愛的鳥類祖先：

「是啊，我也像你們說的……」

人類祖先看大家意見一致，於是鄭重宣布：

「那麼，大家從現在開始品嚐萬物，把最符合自己口味的東西當作永遠的食物吧！」

這話一說完，大家便爭先恐後品嚐地上所有的東西。

今天我們人類、獸類、蛇類、鳥類的食物，是這時候約定的結果。

於是，人類的祖先選擇小米與肉。小米的話，是把一粒截成幾塊，將其中一塊放入鍋裡煮，就會有四、五人份的食料。而且，要得到小米不需要耕作廣大田地，只要兩三寸的四方之地，就足夠養活人們。另外，想吃肉的時候，只要呼叫野山豬，拔除其毛，將那根毛剪成幾段，同樣放入鍋裡煮，就會有一大盤美味的肉。比起我們現代嘶吼「給我們麵包！」那可真是極樂世界啊！

閒話至此，如此從木石二質的老樹誕生的人類祖先，先是母子相交、手足交合，像這樣繁殖許多子孫，幾年不到就形成了兩個部落。某日，這甲乙二社，隔著一條河齊聲大喊，以聲音大小比較人數多寡。結果甲社的聲音壓過乙社的聲音，連山岳都為其轟然之聲而震動。他們趁勢向乙社的人吶喊：

「你們看我們這威力，我們不想跟你們住在同一個地方。我們要下山去平地。你們刺青跟我們做區分吧！如果你們不喜歡這個差別，儘管來獵我們的人頭吧！我們是多數，不會怕你們的。」

筆者本來以為，人種歧視這種東西是美國的專利，但沒想到蕃人從神代就產生這樣的問題。若他們美國人聽到這個故事，應該會覺得找到知音而會心一笑吧。來到平地的，是今天臺灣人的祖先，而留在山上的，是今天有幸改稱為高砂族的蕃人祖先。就這樣，神代在此平靜落幕。

取得火種的故事

　　高砂族的先祖時代沒有火，食物皆生吃，夜晚也沒有燈火，極為不便。於是有一天，部落的有力者聚集起來舉行協議會，但絞盡腦汁也想不出什麼好主意。因此人們分頭各自尋找火種。有人登高山，有人入深谷，雖歷經千辛萬苦，卻都徒勞無功。人們很失望，在山頂露宿過夜。到了深夜，有一人激動大聲喊叫：

　　「看到火了！看到火了！」

　　人們聽到這個聲音，從臥睡的草地跳起，眺望遠方的海面，看到離岸很遠的海上有一個閃亮的火影。

　　「太好了！」

　　大家不約而同齊聲歡呼，但那是離陸地遙遠的海上，沒有人前往。因此，首先差遣以沉著勇敢聞名的熊，但可憐牠因為激浪，在途中就沉入海底。接著派出以勇猛著稱的豹，然而牠也被巨浪吞噬。人們見狀，發出絕望的哀嘆。此時出現一隻羌仔，牠說：

　　「各位，請派我去取火種吧。平日被其他野獸侮辱的我，就算拚了命也要完成這個使命。」

　　眾人聽了這很有男子氣概的話，便決定派遣羌仔前往。牠志氣昂揚、勇敢無懼，如飛鳥般投入海裡，不畏如山般席捲而來的海浪，在水裡載沉載浮，終於取得火種歸來。大家都高興極了。

　　「啊！勇敢而可愛的羌仔啊！」

　　人們一面道謝，一面撫摸牠的背，於是牠的毛發出滑潤光澤，變得像今日一般美麗。這個故事告訴我們，平常遭人責罵卻能隱忍自重的人，一旦有事發生，往往能夠發揮很大的力量。這不能單單視為是原始時代幼稚的童話故事。

搗蛋神的故事

　　世上有什麼東西是麻煩的呢？再也沒有比變化自如的搗蛋神更麻煩了。是的，他利用不可思議的神力為難正直的人類，真是豈有此理。

　　從前從前高天原有位叫作 Idotsuku（イドツク）的神。有天他百無聊賴地從雲間窺探下界，清楚看到人們生活在那裡。

　　「這真有趣，我也加入人類好了！」

　　Idotsuku 這麼說，便從天上大剌剌降地臨到地上。他來到太巴塱蕃社，娶了一位名叫 Rume（ルメ）的美麗女子為妻。然而，不知他

在想什麼，某日又再度升天，不久後帶回來兩節竹子和兩個 papaku
（パパク）。從那之後，他便不下田，躲在幽暗屋裡的一個房間，專
心捲繞著絲線。不僅家人見狀感到奇怪，就連鄰居們只要一碰面，也
會嘲笑 Idotsuku 的愚蠢。

「雖說是從天上降臨的神，但光繞著絲線也沒飯吃吧！」

「俗話說笨蛋無藥醫，說的就是 Idotsuku 哪。」

「所以他是被其他神放逐，流浪到下界的吧，哈哈哈哈……」

把這些人的話當作馬耳東風的 Idotsuku，不久即捲出千尋的絲
線[1]。他獨自上山，在各處打樁，把自己捲繞的絲線綁在木樁上，並
將末端綁在山腳下，然後用力一拔。結果，不可思議的，隨著宛如瞬
間落下百雷般的巨響，原本蒼鬱的樹木被悉數拉倒。Idotsuku 等這些
樹木枯萎後，放了把火將它們燒光。然後他站在火燒後的荒地上玩陀
螺，並把沒有燒完的殘株丟向人們的田地。

「把殘株丟到別人的田地實在太過分了，Idotsuku 是神，不懂人
道。」

田地的主人這麼叫嚷著，但害怕其神術的人們，還是無法當著他
的面做什麼。於是到了夜晚，他們偷偷上山，把那些殘株丟回
Idotsuku 的田地，然後若無其事回家。隔天早上見狀的 Idotsuku，站
在那裡撒尿，把這些殘株又沖回人們的田地，然後隨即在這些地方撒
上夕顏花的種子。這時，他的岳父看不下去，對他說：

「Idotsuku 啊，我敬佩您的神術，但聰明如你，卻偏偏撒了夕顏
種子，是怎麼一回事？拜託你撒米或小米的種子吧！」

「父親大人！請稍候一段時間，然後等待收穫的喜悅吧！」

就這樣，到了夕顏花盛開時，Idotsuku 蓋了十座穀倉。什麼也不

1　譯者註：一尋＝1.515公尺至1.816公尺。

知道的岳母[2]，其女人情緒對 Idotsuku 的瘋狂行徑感到忍無可忍，於是藏身起來不再露面。然而 Idotsuku 對這些事情毫不在乎，然後自己來到院子鋪下草席，在上面搖晃身體，他的體毛掉下後全都變成人類。他莞爾而笑，帶著這些人上山，採收纍纍的夕顏果實回家，以蕃刀剖開果實。結果，從一粒籽中，湧出四、五升的小米[3]，轉眼間在院子裡堆成一座小米山，十個穀倉裡都充滿金黃色的小米。

「嘿，現在我要來懲罰嘲笑我的傢伙了。」

Idotsuku 一邊自言自語，一邊來到海岸。在那裡捕魚的人們正在分配獲物。凡是 Idotsuku 大搖大擺行經之處，很不可思議的，原本活蹦亂跳的魚瞬間都變成了黑石。大家又驚又怕，哭著拉他袖子，為過去的所言所行道歉。結果那些黑石轉眼又變回原本的魚。據說這時殘餘的黑石就是今天的石炭。

有一天，部落的人從耕地回家的路上，看到美麗的木材掉在路上，於是很高興將它帶回去，正要從肩上卸下來時，木材就變成了 Idotsuku。

「謝謝！因為我太累了，躺在路旁，託你的福，把我扛在肩上帶到這裡，我才不用走那累人的山路，真的很謝謝你。」

還有一天，Idotsuku 變成漂流木漂到河岸邊，有人正要拾起時，突然就變回了 Idotsuku，在那裡吟吟笑著。又有一次，他在人們耕作的地方變身成鹿奔跑，人們丟下鋤頭追他，他便跑到人們身後，把鋤頭藏在草叢裡，然後若無其事的回家。諸如此類的惡作劇，人人都束手無策。

不過，在一個電光閃爍、雷鳴轟然的日子，Idotsuku 第三度升天，從此再也沒有回來下界了，人們是多麼開心。直到今天，他們蕃

2　譯者註：原文為「養母」。
3　譯者註：一升＝1.8公升。

人不侵犯其他人的境界，不丟塵埃，小米收穫的時候，殺豬殺雞祭拜祖先與 Idotsuku。另外，捕魚時若有其他人經過的話，一定會把漁獲分配給他們等等。被形容是慓悍無比的高砂族，竟然拿 Idotsuku 的惡作劇毫無辦法，真是趣味無窮的人類生活啊！

女護島的故事

從前有位漁夫，在一個悠然的春日，他升起竹筏的風帆，划著划著，便划向了外海，但不知為何，那天一條魚也釣不到。他很失望，把釣竿丟向船緣，茫然眺望海面，那裡浮著一座烏黑的小島。

「啊！好美的島！去那個島上休息一下好了。」

他立刻將竹筏划過去，大剌剌地登上那座島。然後一邊自言自語的說：「這樣真好！」，一邊從腰邊拿出煙草盒。結果，不可思議的，突然驚覺那座小島開始動了起來，旋即從腳下傳來巨大的聲響。

「喂！是哪個傢伙趁我午睡時在我背上抽煙啊？」

「嚇我一跳！島先生，你竟然跟人一樣會講話。」

「喂喂，開什麼玩笑。我不是島，我是鯨魚先生，你這個笨蛋。」

鯨魚這麼怒吼，然後生氣地搖擺身體，漁夫便被甩到不知幾百里遠的國度。那是一個他從來沒聽過、也沒看過的異鄉之地。而且他的周圍盡是女人，那些女人們好奇打量著他，不久便開始這樣的對話。

「這是什麼？」

「看起來是人類的形狀，但跟我們不一樣，顏色黑黑的，骨架和肉身較大，是畸形的不祥動物吧。」

「啊！這會不會是我們在古老傳說裡聽過的豬，我們一起把他抓來飼養吧。」

那個漁夫聽了一驚，雖說顏色黝黑，竟然把人當作豬，他感到很悲哀，眼淚撲簌簌落下並哭了出來。但那些女人們完全不理會他的哭泣，將他關在小屋裡，每天只有給他剩飯和切剩的芋頭等。過沒多久，消瘦衰弱下來的他，趁女人們沉睡時偷偷來到海岸。然後遠眺月光下遙遠的彼方，想到自己再也回不去令人懷念的故鄉，不禁潸然淚下。結果，之前的那隻鯨魚又再度慵懶地浮出海面，漁夫看到牠，便合掌向鯨魚說：

「鯨魚先生，拜你所賜，我吃了很大的苦頭。拜託你，請讓我再次回到故鄉吧。」

「真是可憐！你坐到我背上來吧，我馬上送你回去。」

漁夫按照鯨魚的指示跳到牠背上，然後鯨魚把尾巴搖擺了兩三下，他眼前立刻出現令人思念的故鄉。

「啊！看到陸地了，看到故鄉的森林了！」

他歡欣鼓舞，鯨魚告訴他：

「喂，人類先生，你回到家之後，請你給我一點供品吧。」

「你是我的救命恩人，我已經有我的打算了。」

「那就這麼約定嘍！」

才聽到咚隆一聲巨響，他就已經被甩上陸地了。狂喜的他立刻返回家，牽起妻子和小孩的手，高興得哭了起來。

「啊，夫君，我們多麼擔心你，真高興你回來了。」

「對不起，讓你們擔心了，我被鯨魚送去可怕的女護島。」

「女護島！」

「不要誤會，雖然那是只有女人的島，不過我在那裡被當作豬，被迫只吃剩飯與切剩的芋頭。」

「竟然把我重要的丈夫當作豬……」

「別生氣，我就是因為被當作豬，才能這樣回來。」

妻子聽到「女護島」而燃起嫉妒之心，又因聽到「被當作豬」而憤怒，不過最後因為丈夫的話終於露出了笑容。

「真的很高興，對我來說是親愛的丈夫，對孩子來說是重要的父親，這樣的人，現在平安歸來了。」

妻子陷入忘我的情緒，高興地轉圈迴旋。

「啊，對了，我不能這樣怠慢，我和鯨魚有重要的約定……」

於是，他再度回到海岸，在那裡鋪設草席，其上放了酒、餅、檳榔子等靜候鯨魚。不久，彷彿才看到遙遠彼方波浪間出現那隻鯨魚，海水便捲起巨浪將供品吞噬而去，唯獨草席留在海濱，如今變成了起起伏伏的海浪。此外，據聞搭在臺灣本島與火燒島之間的美麗大橋這時掉落海裡，變成了像今天一樣各自獨立的島嶼。

（原刊於《臺灣警察協會雜誌》第87號，1924年8月25日）

輯二

傳說的高砂族（二）

征伐太陽的故事

住在寒帶和溫帶地區的人因為害怕寒冷，所以極為尊敬熾盛有熱力的太陽，將其視為主神，把照亮黑夜的月亮視為從神。而住在熱帶及亞熱帶地區的人則相反，厭惡酷暑，崇敬夜間皎潔月光的清朗，將其視為主神，而太陽是從神。至於極端酷暑之地，甚至還會敵視太陽。本故事的起源即來自於此。

太古時代有兩個太陽，不分晝夜熾烈照耀，結果溪流乾涸，田園荒廢，糧食斷絕，可憐的人們束手無策，只好等待餓死。在絕境時依靠神是人之常情，不分國之東西、時之古今。但人們雖向神祈禱求救了，不幸卻毫無效果。

「神應該要解救我們的悲慘困境啊，我們一起以赤誠祈願，但神卻沒有應許我們，祂是多麼無情……」

群眾裡有一人以熱烈語氣如此呼喊，大家也激動地吶喊附和他。

「是的，我們不應該再依賴這種沒有慈悲心的神，我們自己的事，應該要由我們自己解決。」

「醒來吧，同胞們！起來吧，諸君！」

人們的情緒高昂到了極點，殺氣充滿天地，被沸然的氣氛包圍。此刻，兩位青年推開群眾走到前面，然後說：

「諸君！請勿擔憂，我們兩人現在就去射殺太陽。希望各位忍受短暫的痛苦，等待今日的悲憤化為歡喜的日子到來。」

話說完，這兩位青年便帶著小米與朱藥，英勇走向征伐太陽的旅途。長途跋涉幾萬里，歷經星霜幾十年，他們在辛苦艱難中終於抵達世界的邊界。志氣昂揚、勇敢無懼的兩位青年站在崖邊，拉開弓箭，迫不及待地等候太陽的升起。不久後，熾烈宛若熔鐵般的赤紅太陽出現在海的彼方。勇敢的兩青年，抓緊機會迅速射出箭，兩支箭毫無偏差射中了太陽中心。場面悲壯悽慘，眼見淋漓鮮血如急流般落下，海上泛著紅色浪潮。可憐的是，其中一位青年被太陽的血沖進海裡而喪命。倖存的那位青年毫無射落太陽的喜悅，在失去同伴的悲傷裡，悄然一個人寂寞地踏上歸途。兩人在征途的路上所丟下的朱藥果實，如今已長成大樹，樹上果實纍纍，青年將它當作已故友人的悲傷回憶，循著這個路標，終於回到家鄉。當初送青年出征的父母已不在世，在門口迎接的老人是他的朋友，他訝異之餘，心裡感念父母在世時的種種。

「迎接我們的救命恩人吧！」

「我們多虧這位恩人才得到夜晚，得到了涼爽；有了夜晚，人生才是快樂的；有了涼爽，作物才會結果。」

「是啊！讓這個光榮的功績流傳千古吧。」

在皎潔的月光下，人們帶著歡喜與感謝舉杯互敬暢飲，一位老翁站在臺上仰天說道：

「諸君！諸君知不知道現在我們頭上閃亮的月亮與星星啊。在曾經有兩個太陽而沒有夜晚的過去，在天上照耀的，只有讓我們痛苦的太陽。然而，這位勇敢的青年，射落一個太陽時，散落四方的血潮留在天上成為了月亮與星星。今晚，我們可以享受月光的清朗與欣賞星座的美麗，全是拜這位青年所賜。」

掌聲如雷響起。就在涼風不停吹來清香的綠蔭下，狂歡的人們忘記時間已晚，不斷舉杯慶祝。

日、月、星的故事

父親砍倒了據說有樹靈的巨大老檜，鬆了口氣，不久便對專心搬運的兒子們說：

「總覺得渴到不行，你們去溪邊取水過來吧。」

兄弟聽從父親的命令，帶著竹筒往溪谷間走去，但平常潺湲清澈的溪流，卻在這天，沒有降雨竟也烏黑混濁。兄弟看到這水流雖感訝異，但也未繼續深究，便空手回去告訴父親。父親只是苦笑，沒有回答。不久太陽便西沉，這天也結束了。翌日，他們又按照父親的命令去溪邊，溪流仍然像前日一樣混濁。又過了一天，他們第三度前往，水卻愈發混濁。父親聽到兄弟的報告之後，皺起眉頭，片刻後靜靜開口：

「那一定是因為上游有惡作劇的人。是牛？是豬？還是人？你們兩個去，不用手下留情，把他的頭砍下吧。」

於是，兄弟心氣昂揚地前往溪谷間，接著往上游溯尋，果然如父親所說，那裡有一個男人，將頭夾在股間，正在弄濁溪水。兄弟見狀，趁他不注意時，憤怒地將他打倒馘首。但仔細一看，這是怎麼一回事？那個人頭竟是命令他們砍頭的父親。兄弟知情後，又是驚訝得

快發狂，又是哀嘆悲傷，但事到如今也無可奈何。他們哭著回家告訴母親，母親說：

「你們既然有獵父親人頭的勇氣，那獵別人的頭應該就很容易吧。去吧，現在立刻去馘首吧！在獵到數百個人頭之前，不准回家……」

母親帶著怒氣粗暴地把兄弟趕出門。兩人俯首淚下，不久，弟弟撫摸哥哥的肩膀說：

「哥，既然如此，我們就必須聽從母親大人的話，多獵人頭，至少要安慰已故父親大人之靈，並解除母親大人對我們的責罰才行。聽說卑南社的人們勇猛，只要看見敵人，就是天涯海角也會追到底，我們去利用他們的特性，將他們誘引到加納納谷，然後設石柵一舉獵得數十個人頭吧！」

「喔喔，老弟！你的主意真不錯。那我們即刻出征吧。」

於是兄弟兩人在深山幽谷裡獵殺豹，帶著牠的血前往卑南社，確認蕃童正熟睡，便出其不意開槍，打中其中三人。聽到突如其來的槍聲而驚醒的蕃社人們，馬上發現兄弟，於是帶著槍械前來追捕。兄弟心想成功了，將帶來的豹血滴在逃跑的路上，假裝他們負傷，以誘導他們。同時在溪流兩岸，像橋一樣地掛上藤，其上安置大石，再一口氣將籐切斷，隨著轟然巨響，一舉殺了追捕而來的數十人。他們帶著這些人頭回家，供在父親的亡靈前，並向母親謝罪，與妹妹一同在靈前舞蹈。

結果，不可思議的，兄弟妹二人先是腳掌沒入地下，接著是小腿淹沒，甚至及腰。就這樣身體逐漸沉到地下，連人頭都快要淹沒的時候，三人齊聲向母親說：

「我們如願祭拜父親大人的亡靈，安慰母親大人的心，已經沒有任何遺言要說，那麼，我們就這樣一邊唱歌跳舞，一邊沉入地下。今

晚躍升山頂上的月亮，是哥哥。明早升至東方天空的，是弟弟（在此不可忽略的是像〈征伐太陽的故事〉一樣，以月為主，以日為從）。而在天空中的幽暗裡閃亮的大星星，是妹妹。那麼母親大人，祝您永遠健康快樂……」

不久後，三個人一邊唱歌，一邊沉入地底。冬天日落較早，暮藹煙霞瀰漫時，東邊山岳邊緣出現皎潔的月亮，須臾片刻後，光亮柔和的星星也開始閃耀，雞鳴抖擻報曉時，熾盛的太陽便在東方天空升起。……據聞像這樣一個月一次，哥哥的月亮，與弟弟的太陽，會互相接近問候對方，這個無盡的過程將永遠循環下去。

變成雷電的故事

　　從前在某個山村裡，住著一戶感情和睦的親子三人。但有一日，那對父子一早出門打獵後，直到傍晚都沒有歸來。母親在昏暗的燈火下，擔心他們是不是被可怕的怪獸吃掉了？還是掉入深溪？其女人特有的心緒擔憂著丈夫與孩子。到了夜晚，兒子一人悄然歸來。

　　「啊，你終於回來了。媽媽多麼擔心你。來，快上來吧。咦？你父親呢……」

　　被問及父親時，兒子抽抽搭搭哭了出來。

　　「我們兩人迷路了，結果我找不到父親，就這樣好不容易一個人回到這裡。」

　　「什麼！你把父親獨自丟在山上一個人回來？你這個不孝子。就算看不到父親，叫喊他的名字，也應該會有回應吧……」

　　「沒有，我叫了好幾次了，都沒有父親的回應。」

　　母親聽了這話後怒氣沖沖，獨自將火把點上，衝進夜霧裡去尋找丈夫。然後終於在一個溪谷間找到丈夫，她狂喜地擁抱丈夫。

　　「啊，你活著真好！那個不孝子真是的！」

　　父親回到家，因為聽了妻子的報告，於是粗聲責罵：

　　「你這個不孝子，你說你叫我，我沒有回應，難道我這個父親的

聲音傳不到你耳裡嗎？這聲音響遍整座山！你這麼大聲呼喊，我這個父親怎麼可能不回應。聽吧！這個聲音、這個聲音！」

他大肆咆哮後，便牽著母親的手升天了。在那之後，父親變成雷，母親則變成電。也就是說，那時候父親的聲音是雷鳴，母親的火把是電光，此說流傳至今。

舉天王鳥的故事

高砂族祖先的時代，天就在不遠的地方，人們無法到地面上，只好在地下挖掘洞穴生活。因為這樣極為痛苦不便，無論如何都想在廣大的地面上愉快生活，於是有天他們召開協議會。然而，沒有人願意出來完成這個任務，席間只是迴盪著深沉的嘆息。結果末座有位少年走上前開口說道：

「要去除太陽的苦熱，除了把天舉高之外別無他法。為此，住在地面上的我們人類和獸類，是毫無用處的。完成此重責大任的，除了在天空遨翔的鳥類之外，沒有別的了。希望先召集所有的鳥，再進一步想出更好的辦法。」

大家不禁為這個少年的奇智鼓掌喝采，於是長老向天上大聲呼喊：

「全世界所有的鳥兒們！你們趕快過來參與我們謀劃的事吧！」

聽到這聲音的鳥兒們好奇是怎麼回事，爭先恐後聚集到人們面前。於是長老嚴肅地告訴牠們：

「鳥兒們！如你們所見，今天的天地距離非常近，每天因太陽而焦死者多得數不清。因此，我們也像這般在地下挖洞生活。我想你們也不希望有這樣的痛苦與不便。是的，如果天高一點的話，你們就可以盡情遨翔雲際。我們也可以自由走出地面。為了我們和你們，請把天舉高，讓大家脫離這種熾烈炎熱之苦吧。」

於是，首先第一個出現的是老鷹。

「那是舉手之勞。我只要在空中振翅二三次，就可以把天搧飛到高處去。」

高傲的老鷹這般大言壯語，然後飛衝上天啪嗒啪嗒地振翅，但天毫無驚慌之貌。於是老鷹搔搔頭飛了下來。接著出現的是烏鴉。

「哈哈哈哈……各位，看看這位說得到做不到的老鷹君的樣子吧。我原本在太陽裡生活，所以身體才如此焦黑，我跟太陽交情就是這麼好。那麼我就直接找他商量去吧。」

於是烏鴉飛向太陽，但過了很久都沒有回來。

「烏鴉果然也不行哪！」

人們面帶愁容。剛剛的那位少年也面露不安之色，環視在場的鳥兒們。結果在那裡，有隻名叫 Tatachiyu（タタチユ）的小小鳥兒，小步小步走了出來。其他的鳥兒們見狀，互相拉拉袖子……喔不，是翅膀，嘲笑著牠。

「看，笨蛋無藥醫。那個小呆子 Tatachiyu 竟然厚著臉皮走出去。」

「真是沒有自知之明的 Tatachiyu，不知羞恥也不知別人怎麼想，倒覺得牠這樣很可憐。連那勇猛的老鷹君都失敗了，而且就算是跟太陽感情極好的烏鴉君也沒有平安回來……」

Tatachiyu 對這些鳥兒們的嘲笑聽若未聞，接著以牠可愛的小小身體，使出渾身力量啼叫：「他啾卡、他啾卡、他啾卡……」。那個聲音清亮、純淨、遼朗。人們忘我地沉醉。結果這聲音逐漸往四方傳

響擴散，天地為之震動，天便迅速地往上層升去。

　　現在我們能夠在地面上安穩生活，實是拜小鳥所賜。於是這 Tatachiyu 成為萬鳥之王，歷經幾千年星霜，直到今天，被尊為神鳥而受到崇敬。

風、雨、雪的故事

　　有一天，風、雨、雪聚在一起，開始誇耀自己的力量。

　　「在這世上，應該沒有像我力量這麼強大的了。凡是我所到之處，宇宙萬物沒有不風靡的。」

　　首先這麼說，然後高傲地抬起不怎麼高的鼻子抽動著的，是風。其後，搶著接話的是雨。

　　「我沒有像風君那麼粗魯，不過，這個漸漸滲透土地的力量，連大山都能崩解。比起我們，雪君只有像女人般的白臉，完全不行吧！」

　　「是啊，雪君作為我們的朋友，實在太過貧弱，哈哈哈哈……」

　　雪默默聽著雨和風的嘲笑，這時首度開口。

　　「我的身體的確像女人般的白，而且不像風君一樣無法捕捉，也不像雨君一樣潮濕陰沉。凡是我所到之處，全都變成銀色世界，那樣的寒冽一定是刺骨的。依我來看，你們的力量只不過是小把戲。」

　　雨和風聽到這話後，面紅耳赤，憤怒異常。

　　「好吧！那我們來實際較量三人的力量吧。」

　　心急的風話一說完，便卯足丹田用力一吹。結果天地為之鳴動，石飛樹倒，雲像急流般飄動，呈現出相當駭人的光景。

　　「喂！看我的厲害，我的力量很偉大吧，哈哈哈哈……。雨君，你也大顯身手嚇嚇雪這傢伙吧。」

　　雨說了聲好啊，便沛然落下，瞬間溪谷暴漲，濁流如瀑布般往下沖。

　　「嘿嘿嘿嘿，雨君的本事真是令人佩服。」

　　風雖然鼓掌，但還是說著這種惹人厭的話。雪笑吟吟地看著他們的樣子，這時輪到自己了，他靜靜地、沉沉地，如灑白羽般落下。結果原本青蔥的草木瞬間枯萎，望眼山野，所見之處無不白皚一片，水結冰，薯物結凍，身體逐漸冰冷，原本在巖窟裡嘲笑風雨的高傲的人們，害怕顫抖，最後跪在雪前。見狀的風雨，原先的氣勢都不見了，偷偷摸摸地逃走。

　　住在高山不知害怕風雨的高砂族，是多麼害怕寒冷，從這個小故事裡可以窺知。

　　　　　　（原刊於《臺灣警察協會雜誌》第88號，1924年9月25日）

輯三

傳說的高砂族（三）

開始狩首的故事

　　天皇在位，光芒普照大地，連南溟孤島深山的雜草都能蒙受惠澤，實是可貴。距今三千年的過去，一位叫作 Nibunu（ニブヌ）的神降臨新高山，在此首度創造人類。當時的人類，由於是神親手所造，極為純潔，被允許擁有幾近不老不死的長壽。因此，倘若不小心喪命，也能依靠 Nibunu 的神力復活。而這樣勞煩神力多達五次後，就被視為在這世上已無用處而遭到放棄。那或許是因為即使不小心，但連續喪命五次的人，神便認為他不珍惜生命，因而拋棄他吧。

　　閒話休題，有一天 Nibunu 神因為有急事，把一個第二次喪命的人直接留在家中便出門了。其後，一位叫作 Soesoha（ソエソハ）、非常好管閒事的神來到祂家，抱著亡者痛哭不已，於是在那個家裡挖洞將屍體埋葬，覆蓋土於其上，然後倒伏哭泣。事情忙完回到家中的 Nibunu 見這光景大吃一驚，但因為 Soesoha 神已經哭了，所以無可奈何。星霜推移三千年，他們將死者埋在家裡，在上面悲泣的習慣，至今仍沒有改變。

　　從此之後，人類擁有任何時候都可能即刻死亡的光榮。但因為人類繁殖能力實在驚人，其粗製濫造的結果，產出了性質不佳的傢伙。因此 Nibunu 神為了去除這些惡人而降下大洪水，使四方瀰漫濁水。結果丘陵也瞬間被濁水吞噬，人們好不容易才逃跑，再度聚於新高山頂。

「真是駭人的水。」

「望眼之處都是濁流狂奔，這不是很令人愉快嗎？」

「喂喂！不要在那裡說不停，會得罪神喔。」

那個時候，就已經有插科打諢的吊兒郎當之人了，也有把神視為萬能而行為神經質的人。

「肚子餓了呀。」

一個人忽然想起似地這麼說，其他人就抱著肚子附和說：「餓了呀」。當時沒有穀類，而是狩獵野獸作為常食，因此在此大水的情況下，根本無法覓食。於是一個壯者殺死自己飼養的狗。剛剛插科打諢的那個人見狀，便將狗頭插在竹竿上，在人們之間揮舞行走著。雖然其中也有人皺起眉，但許多人都覺得很有趣而歡快地鼓掌。

「你看那竹竿上的狗頭。」

「雖然只有頭，卻像樣地睜著眼耶。」

「沒有身體反而很奇特很有趣呢。」

那位打諢之人聽了人們的話之後，愈發得意忘形，這次殺了猴子，將猴頭與狗頭交換。人們愈來愈感到有趣，讚賞他的新奇。

「光是猴頭就這麼有趣，若這是我們人類的頭，會多麼的好玩呢！」

「哼，過去很囂張跋扈的傢伙突然死掉，將其蒼白的臉曬在竹竿前端，不知會多麼痛快。」

「好玩、好玩！」

已經充滿殺氣的眾人，把當時部落裡被憎惡的惡童殺死，並將他的頭插在竹尖，忘我地瘋狂跳舞。或許這馘首舞符合神意，大水轉瞬減退，丘陵和原野都再度重現眼前。

「水已經退了，我們前去良地吧。然後我們組一隊伍，狩集其他部落人的首級吧。連我們部落人的頭都這麼有趣的話，不知獵敵人的

頭會有多麼愉快。」

　　人人手上拿著武器，衝向黎明的雲霧，離開了新高山。

開始分家的故事

　　從前有一個很孝順的年輕獵人，名叫 Tomaikoru（トマイコール）。無論颱風的早晨，或下雨的傍晚，他都會上山狩獵，同時也下田耕作，並將其所獲獻給父親，他將此事視為最大的喜悅。某日，他一如往常扛著槍械，踏著星光出門，那天早上，霧像雲般深深包圍著山路。一邊喘氣、一邊登山的他，吸入那些霧氣，不禁打了一個噴嚏。結果，在霧中有個人同樣打了噴嚏。

　　「咦？這山裡應該除了我之外，沒有其他人才對，剛剛的噴嚏真奇怪哪。」

Tomaikoru 一個人自言自語，一邊探看四方，但仍未見人影。

「奇怪哪！」

此時，在霧中又聽見同一句話。他循著這個聲音尋找對方，結果彼處有棵盛開怒放的百日紅。Tomaikoru 站在那前面，凝視著花，不久對其開口：

「原來剛剛模仿我講話的是你啊。」

結果，百日紅同樣回覆「原來剛剛模仿我講話的是你啊。」聽了這話的他又說：

「你這樹淨模仿人話到底想做什麼！」

話沒說完，他便拔起腰邊的刀，結果紛紛散落的百日紅花朵中，傳出了一個聲音：

「請等一下……」

「年輕的大人！就算砍樹也請不要傷害我。」

此時他才發現樹中有人，他把百日紅從根砍倒。果然從切口處出現一位美麗女子。

「咦？您怎麼會在這裡？」

Tomaikoru 感到詫異，美麗的女子莞爾而笑說：

「我，是這個百日紅的精靈啊。我一直希望到這世界來，不過無論如何都無法離開這棵樹。結果今天多虧了您，完成我一直以來的心願，沒有什麼事比這更令人高興的了。為了報恩，我要當您的……不，請您允許，讓我當您的妻子。」

於是在百日紅散滿地的樹下，他們結為夫婦，並就地搭造一個簡單樸素的草庵。然而孝順的 Tomaikoru，沒有為了夫婦愛而忘記父親。無論早晨或傍晚，他都會從這個草庵涉溪回父親家，在那裡耕作，然後到了夜晚，再返回愛妻等待的草庵。見狀的父親感到非常不捨，有一天把他叫來膝前，說道：

「Tomaikoru 啊，你無微不至的孝行，我這個做父親的非常清楚。但你不用再像過去那樣每天回父親家了。像最近下大雨，溪水應該會暴漲。不管怎麼說這實在太危險了。所以，以後如果你在山上獵到鹿的話，再把牠的頭帶過來就好。你們兩人永遠相親相愛生活，這就是對我這個父親最好的孝行。」

Tomaikoru 往後只要抓到鹿，一定會探訪父親的家，然後那天就在父親家度過。歲月如流水般逝去，Tomaikoru 如今已年邁，連涉溪都有困難。因此父親送他一個神像，命他出去打獵時，以野獸的頭骨祭拜神，於是父子便完全分開為兩個獨立的家，靜靜度完餘生。據說這是他們高砂族開始分家的由來。

獨木舟的故事

關於漂浮於現今成為臺灣電力株式會社施工的問題中心、自太古以來湛滿碧水的日月潭上的獨木舟，流傳著這樣的故事。

從前從前有五個感情極好的青年。有一天，這五人一起深入中央山脈狩獵，但不知為何，那天連一隻獵物都沒有。但太陽已毫不留情西傾了，蕃山的山壁瀰漫紫色煙霞。筋疲力盡的五人，坐在某個大岩石上，茫然眺望夕陽西下的景色。然後，五人宛若融入深山的沉默般閉口無言。就在那時，不知道從何處來的一隻白鹿，電光般從他們面前跑了過去。原先動也不動的五個年輕人，見狀後馬上起身追捕，白鹿最後跑到日月潭，然後如飛鳥般跳進水裡，又沉又浮游到湖上的浮島。年輕人站在湖邊，像作夢一樣凝視水面，不可思議的，在那裡出現坐在樟楠木片上的老鼠。五個年輕人看到牠，終於首度開口：

「喂喂！水上的老鼠先生，你為什麼坐在那小小木片上都不會沉下去？你是怎麼往前的呢？」

老鼠聽到年輕人的聲音，回頭瞪了一眼，但始終保持沉默，將自己的尾巴當作船舵，往前划啊划的。

「真不可思議啊。」

「到底怎麼做才能浮在這麼深的水上？」

「水深不知幾百尺的湖泊，怎麼橫渡啊？」

「不對，那是神。千萬別懷疑。」

「是的，我們模仿那位神的啟示，橫渡這個湖吧。」

於是五人便刳剖大樹製作木舟，削木板製作船舵，讓它漂浮在夕陽映照的潭水上，木舟在湧來的小波中靜靜搖晃著。五個年輕人興致高昂地跳上木舟，這個輕飄飄的感覺，對在山岳裡赤腳爬上爬下的他們來說，有著從未體驗過的愉快。年輕人們像小孩般興高采烈，一邊划著船側的水，一邊迅速來到浮島。然後順利捕捉到先前逃跑的白鹿，回到原來的岸邊。有一個土人在樹間窺見這一切，等年輕人們從木舟上來後，便跑出來對他們說：

「那個東西非常方便呢，請問可以讓給我嗎？」

「喂，是怎麼了，突然講得這麼大聲。」

「啊，失禮。其實，我想你們帶著這種東西根本不可能越過那高山回去，所以我這裡帶來很好的肉。來，這個跟你們的木舟交換吧。」

「喂喂，不要把我們當作笨蛋。那種小氣的肉，怎麼能和這個木舟交換？我們沒那麼笨。啊！那個坐船的感覺啊！我們要坐著它回家。」

年輕人一邊這麼說，一邊把木舟拉到陸地上。然後立刻跳上船，不過這次木舟一點也不輕飄飄，完全沒有舒服的感覺。於是他們拚命地划著手，木舟還是絲毫不動。五個年輕人互看彼此，表情像是快哭出來的樣子。土人見狀，使壞說：

「哼，那我要回去了。你們就坐著它越過那高峰回去吧。」

五個年輕人搔搔頭，交換了木舟與肉。然後消失在暮色漸暗的樹林間。至今仍漂浮在那湛藍水面且富有詩意的獨木舟，當水力電力施工完成之際，終將毫無痕跡地消失無蹤吧。

預言者的故事

Kasautamo（カサウタモ）逐漸衰弱，他感覺自己已將不久於人世，便從病床爬起，趴跪在父母面前說：

「父親、母親，謝謝你們長年來的照顧，我終究無法康復並繼續侍奉你們。身為人子，沒有比這更不孝的吧。不過，我絕不會就這樣拋棄父母。假使我的呼吸就這樣斷了，身體變得冰冷，只要右手大拇指仍會動的話，我就一定會重生，對你們盡孝道。萬一手指沒有動靜的話，到那時候，你們就當作我永遠死去了吧……」

他這麼說完，便靜靜閉上眼，睡著般斷了氣。然而，那大拇指不可思議地微微動著。父母雖然深感哀傷，但至少還抱著兒子再生的期待，他們小心呵護照顧他的遺體。從第一天到第三天早上，那手指的活動逐漸微弱，但到了第三天午後，活動稍微變快，到了第五天傍晚，才看到他微微開始呼吸後不久，他便帶著微笑甦醒了。父母與兄弟驚喜萬分，人們包圍著他祝福其再生。

「父親、母親，以及各位兄弟，我五天前斷氣身亡，神從天降臨，呼叫我的名字，並牽起我的手，就這樣帶我升天。我首次看到天上的美麗與珍奇，實在無法言喻。閃亮宮殿中的眾神多麼尊貴。天女身穿金襴輕快跳舞，是多麼美麗。簡直是下界人們連想像都想像不到的佳麗歡樂境！」

「唉呀！你一直跟神在一起嗎？」

「母親，請為我高興。我度過了如夢似幻的五天。」

「你也許過得很開心，但自從你斷氣之後，我們是多麼擔心你啊」

「父親，請您放心。以此為代價，我被傳授了下界人作夢都想不到的奇術。」

「奇術！奇術！」

「各位兄弟，請你們靜靜聽。在剛剛說的綺麗宮殿裡，有個特別顯目威嚴的神把我叫過去，對我說：『你就成為人類的預言者吧。我現在就把必備的奇術傳授給你。』接著便親手將那些神奇的法術傳授給我。於是我離開令人難捨的天國，回到這個下界。」

人們都覺得不可思議，不禁想一窺那樣的奇術，但 Kasautamo 說：「神術是天啟，沒事的話不能施展。」不願輕易施展奇術。然而在那之後，他預知在人界裡將會發生的各種現象，而救人免於災禍，卜知外出打獵時獲物的有無及多寡，並占測一年是豐收或歉收、失蹤者的所在，每每都會說中。

原來這位 Kasautamo，就是預言者的始祖，他們高砂族相信預言占卜是神的奇術。

（原刊於《臺灣警察協會雜誌》第89號，1924年10月25日）

輯四

傳說的高砂族（四）

二神變成鶴的故事

　　從前從前，高天原有一男一女名叫 Madabira（マダビラ）與 Risun（リスン）的神。有一天他們降臨南方某個高嶺，生下四男二女。不過母神懷有次女時，從腹部綻放出燦爛的光，因此體內如水晶般透明。後來足月誕生下來的，果然是不違背此奇蹟，比花還要美麗的女神。父母二神格外寵愛地養育這個次女，歲月如流水般流逝，她已迎來十八歲的春天。某日，她如往常般一個人去谷間取水，不可思議的，那裡佇立著一位從未見過的美少年。女孩見狀想逃跑，他往前抓住她的袖子說：

　　「我絕不是怪人，其實我受海神的命令來迎接您。只有這麼說的話，您可能不懂，其實是海神深切希望迎娶您到他的后宮。五日之後，我會再度來這裡迎接您。懇請您做好準備等候。」

　　話一說完，美少年便突然消失。不知世事、仍很純潔的她，把這件事一五一十告訴父母。父母驚訝無比，立刻製造木箱，把她關在裡面，並緊緊封住蓋子。然而從她體內發出的光，燦爛地穿透那個木箱，洩漏到外頭來。即使再增加二層、三層的木箱，她美麗的樣子仍可從外面一覽無遺。於是他們這次在地下挖洞掩埋她，但燦爛的光仍舊如水晶般照耀那土地。父母兩神坐在上面徹夜不眠守著她，到了第五天傍晚為止，沒有發生任何異狀。於是父母兄弟感到安心，兩個哥

哥出來院子開始搗小米。

　　結果，杵臼的觸擊聲迴響於傍晚的天空，突然烏雲密佈，樹木被風吹得彎下身，瞬間如山般的巨浪席捲而來。房子和人都被這濁流吞沒，幸好他們親子逃到山上。然而，在那些孩子當中，始終沒有看到那心愛的次女。父母二神瘋狂般地呼叫女兒的名字，從山上眺望遙遠彼方的海，結果，很清楚看到她被海神帶走的身影。父母兄弟竭聲大喊，她似乎聽見聲音，回頭遙望山上說：

　　「父親大人，母親大人，以及各位兄弟，我已經覺悟了，一切都是命運。就算現在如何悲傷哭泣，我也無法從海神手中逃離。和父親

大人、母親大人、各位兄弟一起快樂生活的日子，永遠都不會再有了。不過一切都是命運。請你們不要再哭泣。對了，把這個當作紀念吧。」

　　她這麼說完，便切斷自己的手腕投入海裡。結果這手腕變成一條魚，深深游進浪潮裡。

　　「父親大人，母親大人，各位兄弟，我到海神那裡之後，必須每天搗米。我搗米的杵聲，會升天變成雷。今後，看到天上的閃電，聽到雷鳴的話，請你們就把它們當作是我一個人孤伶伶搗米吧。」

　　她美麗的身影就這樣深深沒入海裡。他們全家人一邊瘋狂哭泣，一邊等待水退去，但濁流水勢卻愈來愈大。於是大家翻山越嶺，尋找

前所未見的小米豐收之地。兄弟在途中感到疲累，便留在某個地方，但父母二神仍越過北方的山嶺，終於抵達某個低地。二神把他們的腳踏入這個水地，眺望女兒身影沒入的深藍之海，不可思議的，他們身上長出了翅膀，不知不覺變成了美麗的鶴，朝著天空高飛而去。

因此，據說直到今天都看不到孤鶴，牠們出現時一定是成雙成對飛舞的祥瑞畫面。

少女入月的故事

從前，加禮宛社有一位美麗的女孩。幼時就被繼母養育的她，如世間恆例般，沒有一天不是哭著度日。在她十七歲春天的某日，朋友邀她去附近的海岸拾貝，途中令人難以忍受的臭味不時撲鼻而來。姑娘們笑著罵說：「誰放屁？」到了海岸，太陽早已高高昇起。大家等待退潮的時候，打開隨身攜帶的便當。結果，她的便當雖然外觀是美麗的容器，裡頭竟然裝滿了人糞，大家見狀放聲大笑。

「剛剛路上才覺得很臭，原來便當是糞啊。」

「我都沒有食糞的榮幸呢。」

「糞沒關係啊。任何人的肚子裡都有，呵呵呵呵……」

被其他姑娘們嘲笑的她，不禁面紅耳赤，雙眼撲簌簌地流下熱淚。無心的女孩們看到她可憐的樣子感到過意不去，自責方才毫無同情心，而這樣的心情化為憐憫的眼淚。

「真是可恨的女人。」

「真的是啊，壞心眼也該有限度吧。」

「我們一起來報仇吧……」

原本默默哭泣的她，此時打斷朋友的話，說：

「大家，謝謝妳們的心意。不過這不是母親的錯，是我的

錯⋯⋯。只要我不在家的話，母親一定會成為善良的人。是的，我現在就升天，從此安樂地生活吧。各位，五天之後看看夜晚的月亮，如果看見裡頭有伸著腳、籠子放在一旁，安穩休息的女孩的話，妳們就把她當作我吧。我今天就在這岩石上，等待升上月亮吧。再會了大家！」

女孩們了解她的心情，因此沒有阻止她，她們一邊帶著眼淚互道再見，一邊離開。隔天，她的父親聽到此事，瘋狂般地來到海岸四處尋找，但終究不見可愛女兒的身影。他哭著回家，焦急等待五日後月亮升起，他站上岩石上仰望，看到皎潔月面上可憐女兒的身影。至今部落裡無論老少都在流傳述說她的身影，因此月影總是令人哀傷寂寞的。

少女變成鷲的故事

再來談一個繼母與女兒的悲傷故事吧。有一天，繼母趁丈夫出門打獵，命令女兒 Kaboshi（カボシ）去汲水。Kaboshi 順從聽話地出門，其柔弱的女兒身越過幾重山峰，卻怎麼也找不到可以汲水的溪流。她漸漸感到飢餓，好不容易回到家，跪在母親面前請求說：

「母親大人，我肚子餓得受不了。求求您，給我一碗飯吧。」

繼母聽了之後怒目說：

「給妳這種人的飯一粒也沒有。妳出去汲水太久，所以剩下的飯都餵狗吃了。」

Kaboshi 聽了繼母這番毫無同情的話，脆弱的女兒心終於忍不住，伏身放聲大哭。不久後，心情稍微平靜的 Kaboshi，心想與其侍奉這樣無情的母親，不如變成鳥，自由自在翱翔天空，於是她下定決心。她來到院子，將掃把帶在腰上，兩手拿起竹箕揮了兩三遍，結果不可思議的，可愛的 Kaboshi 突然變成鳥，翩翩停在庭木的小樹枝上。

不知情的父親回家後不見女兒的身影，於是把妻子叫過來詢問。

「Kaboshi 怎麼了？我出門打獵後，因為只有妳和女兒兩個人，所以妳一定知道 Kaboshi 的去處才對。」

聽了丈夫的話，妻子帶著怒氣指著院子的樹木說：

「是的，你可愛的 Kaboshi 變成鳥了。你看，在那樹枝上的，就是不孝 Kaboshi 的下場。」

想都沒過女兒會變成鳥，父親聽了之後十分傷心，哭得痛不欲生，隨即拿著獵到的肉走到那棵樹下，哭著說：

「Kaboshi！Kaboshi！我帶來妳喜歡的肉，求求妳變回原本的樣子吧。」

然而，父親充滿慈愛的話，卑微的鳥是無法理解的，女兒化身的

鳥，翅膀動也不動地瞪著樹下。父親過於悲傷，只是茫然站在那裡，結果不可思議的，父親的頭竟然自己咚的一聲落下。

照理說無情繼母的頭才要咚的一聲落下才對，竟然讓沒有任何罪過的慈父人頭落地，即便是變成鳥類，這種行為也太過卑劣了吧。閒話休題，那個女兒 Kaboshi 化身的鳥，就是今日世上的鷲的祖先。

女人森林的故事

從前有一位年輕獵人，他踏過早晨的露水，進入某個森林深處，那裡有一個從未見過也未聽過的蕃社，蕃社裡盡是美麗的女人。而這些女人們演奏樂器的美妙聲音，在安靜的森林間如夢般迴盪，形成一個難以言喻的神秘世界。年輕獵人在這不可思議的光景裡渾然忘我，茫然凝目注視。這時候，一個女人跟其他女人低聲說了什麼之後，眾女子便如蝴蝶般華麗地包圍住獵人。

「喂喂，年輕獵人先生，您究竟從何處來？」

「我是住在這森林外的人，不小心迷路走到這裡。話說回來，不可思議的是妳們女士們的樣子……」

「呵呵，我們是這個森林的精靈喔。這個森林叫作女人森林，是我們的自由天地，唉呀！您不要那麼驚慌。真是稀客！來，大家，我們來好好來招待這位稀客吧。」

女人們強拉著他的手，將獵人帶進屋裡。所有窗戶都是關著的，不久之後走出走廊的獵人臉色發青，原有的蓬勃生氣都消失殆盡。不過相反的，女人們嘻笑吵鬧，豔麗的弦歌不時打破森林的沉默。

「咦？還想說你去哪裡了？原來你在這裡。」

「年輕獵人先生，我們不會再欺負你了喔，這次真的會好好招待你。」

「真的，真的，跟我們一起……」

她們一邊這麼說，一邊帶獵人去食堂。但不可思議的女人們，只吸蒸氣，對鍋裡的肉和薯，碰也不碰。獵人心想，也許女人們不懂得肉與薯的美味，於是先從鍋子裡夾了一片肉吃。結果女人們臉色一變，互看彼此的臉，然後一個女人不快地說：

「您說您是獵人，是假的吧。您說您是這個森林外的人，全是騙

人吧。」

　　獵人聽到這番令人意外的話，丟下筷子說：

　　「沒有，我不會說謊，我確實是人。」

　　「別再裝了，我們只吸蒸氣與空氣而活，同樣是人類的您，怎麼會吃肉，吃肉的是豬，吃薯的是豬，是的，你是豬！竟然不知道你是豬而招待你，我們真是可悲，我們真是愚蠢……」

　　激憤的女人們，原本的愛意頓時變成憎恨，她們將獵人丟進棚子裡。到了那天夜晚，沒有一個女人靠近那裡。獵人想，一切都是命運，於是繼續保持沉默，但定神一聽，突然聽見不知何處傳來的微弱歌聲。

　　戀人夫妻間怎麼會有謊言呢

　　我的雙眸是活著的

　　如果有謊言的話

　　我手上有刀……

　　這奇異歌聲的主人是誰呢？藉著樹葉間流瀉而下的月光一看，那裡佇立著一位美麗女子。

　　「喂，外來的獵人先生，您在這裡生命有危險，請您趕快逃跑吧。」

　　「啊，請問您……」

　　「噓！聲音太大了。」

　　「您是在我遭受眾女人欺負時，一人寂寞站在遠方樹木後的人！是的，在清澈的眼裡泛著一層霧露的人！這樣的妳，怎麼會來到這裡？」

　　「我原本不是這個森林的女人。不小心迷路走進這個森林，之後變成這森林女人的僕人，如此生活到今天……」

　　「啊！所以妳果然跟我一樣是人！跟我一樣是人！」

「我看到您的身影，開始想念故鄉的父母⋯⋯」

「那是一定的。跟我一起逃離這裡吧。」

「不行，我根本無法逃離，我已經覺悟這一切都是命運。唉呀不好了，屋裡的女人們似乎醒過來了。您再管我的話，您的生命會有危險，請您快逃吧。」

「謝謝，您的恩情，我至死不忘。」

「不用道謝，這都是森林女人們的惡作劇造成的。來吧，快從這柵欄的縫隙逃走吧。」

獵人說著「再會」，快速奔逃而出，他依依不捨回頭看，即使在夜晚的視線裡，還是可以清楚看到黑暗裡她白色的臉⋯⋯。

（原刊於《臺灣警察協會雜誌》第90號，1924年11月25日）

輯五

傳說的高砂族（五）

穿山甲與猴子的故事

　　猴子智慧[1]——有這樣的說法。自古以來人們大都認為猴子有小聰明。在某個山村，住著穿山甲與猴子。有一天，牠們扛著釣竿去附近的河流釣魚，那天大豐收，得到一大籠滿滿的獲物，牠們興高采烈回到家。不過穿山甲口渴得不得了，於是命猴子去取水。猴子立即會意般地出門，不久便帶著竹水筒回來。穿山甲拿到那竹筒，正要喝一口，結果臭氣衝鼻。

　　「喂你！這不是小便嗎？」

　　「不要說傻話了，我才沒有取小便呢。這的確是泉水，為什麼對你來說那麼臭呢？該不會是你自己漏尿吧。通常肚子受涼了，就會不自覺尿出來……」

　　「喂，你到底要取笑我到什麼程度啊。事實勝於雄辯，你來聞聞這惡臭吧！」

　　穿山甲受不了猴子故作糊塗，說完話之後便把竹筒湊到猴子的鼻子前，不過猴子不予理會。穿山甲拿牠沒辦法，不做多想，便自己出去取水了。目送其背影的猴子，露出奸詐的笑容，自言自語說：「人真好騙。」便獨自把籠子裡的魚吃光了，還把穿山甲的箭頭弄鈍，故作不知情的樣子。然後牠對回來的穿山甲說：

1　譯註：日文「猿知惠」是小聰明的意思。

「喂，你不在的時候，一隻大鳥飛來，把魚通通吃掉，我很生氣，想射殺那隻鳥，但不可思議的是那支箭對鳥沒有用，箭頭變得這麼鈍。」

穿山甲聽完奸詐猴子的話，不知在想什麼，拿起一支枴杖，身體輕快地跳上屋頂，又跳回地上。俗話說，猴子喜歡模仿別人，不服輸的猴子，不知自己被設下陷阱，立刻拿起枴杖，像穿山甲一樣跳上跳下，結果滿肚子的魚和糞尿全都爆洩出來。證據確鑿，就算是厚臉皮的猴子，一句抗辯也沒有地認罪了。然而光是這樣穿山甲還是無法息怒。有一天牠們上山燒茅草，心裡打著主意的穿山甲，指著熊熊大火的彼方說：

「誰敢進去那火中呢？你是與生俱來的懦弱者，應該連看火都會害怕吧。」

不服輸的猴子被說成懦弱者，憤怒得全身發抖。

「你辦得到的事情，對我來說也是輕而易舉的事。」

穿山甲聽完猴子的話，就躍進茅草裡，被猴子放的火所包圍。不久後，火一熄，牠便若無其事從灰燼中衝了出來。

「喂，你為什麼沒有燒起來？」

不知道穿山甲潛入地下的猴子，覺得不可思議而這麼問。

「只不過身上穿著乾茅草。」

猴子相信穿山甲的話而模仿他，結果不用說，他再度出現時已變得焦黑。穿山甲剖開焦死猴子的肚子，割除牠的肉，再將其縫回原貌，念了幾句咒語，結果不可思議的，猴子復活了。醒過來的猴子發現自己肚子異常空虛，因此津津有味吃起掉在身旁的肉。見狀的穿山甲一邊罵：「吃自己肉的瘋子！」一邊鑽進土裡。猴子沒辦法，到河岸釣魚，但那天不知為何，一條魚也釣不到。牠茫然凝視著水面，結果出現一個眼睛烏黑的大怪物，猴子沒命似地逃了回去。那時穿山甲

已帶著笑容在家裡等他。

「哈……喂！你為什麼這麼狼狽？」

「唉呀！真是嚇死我了。我從來沒看過那種怪物。」

「啊，那個河的怪物嗎？可能是因為你個性太差，所以水神生氣了。不要再去河邊了，以後兩人一起上山採果實吧！」

「真開心，果然還是知己好。」

隔天，兩人一起上山。那裡有棵大樹，纍纍結滿成熟的紅色果實。猴子迅速從樹幹爬到樹枝上，獨自猛吃著看起來很美味的果實。在樹下等不及的穿山甲對猴子說：

「喂，你給我一個吧。」

「咦？我以為你已經回家了，原來還在那裡。請稍等，給你一個甜的！」

猴子把夾在自己跨下的果實丟下去。不知情的穿山甲很高興，馬上撿來吃了一口，結果一點也不馥郁香甜，而是一股臭氣撲鼻而來。在樹上見狀的猴子放聲哈哈大笑。——所謂宋襄之仁，指的就是穿山甲吧。

開始刺青的故事

太古時代，山野長滿蒼鬱的樹木，在成熟的纍纍果實四季都不間斷的和平世界裡，有一位美麗的女子獨居生活。她早晨在綠蔭下唱歌，夜晚鋪設各種百草為床，有一天，她孕懷大地恩澤，足月後生下一個玉般的男孩。

「真是又小又可愛的孩子……」

她從未看過自己以外的人類，一邊貼著他的臉這麼說，一邊餵他吃美麗的果實。歲月如流水，其後二十年的歲月如夢般流逝。年輕的她，已經是三十五歲的母親，曾經是小小嬰兒的男孩，也成為二十歲的盛年男子。有一天，注視著母親工作的兒子，突然想起什麼似地對母親說：

「母親！妳只有我一個人，不會感到寂寞嗎？我呢，最近因為只有跟母親兩人，總覺得寂寞不堪。」

母親盯著兒子的臉，過了一會兒之後說：

「你啊，真是個膽小鬼。母親雖然是女人身，但出生後十五年間，一直都是一個人生活，自從生下你之後，又過了二十年，說感到寂寞什麼的，連一次也沒有。而你明明是個男人，竟然如此膽小……」

「不過母親，我最近每晚都作夢喔。」

「夢！夢！」

「咦？母親也作夢嗎？我呢，每晚都會做美麗快樂的夢喔。」

「夢！夢！！那個夢是……」

趁母親嗆到時，兒子臉紅地說：

「那是即使在母親面前，也不好意思說的美麗快樂的夢。我呢，從那個夢醒來之後，就感到非常非常寂寞。」

她再也不願意聽下去，心想，我是多麼不懂人情的人哪。因為自己是自然誕生，所以沒有體會過這種感受，不過兒子是從自己肚子裡生出來的，年紀到了，應該會產生戀心。是啊，我得來尋找兒子的伴侶才行。下定決心的她，從翌日起，便每天每天撥開野草，穿梭在山裡的樹林間尋找，但是一個女人都找不到。失望的她，坐在某個岩石上思索什麼似的，不久後，她突然拍了一下膝蓋，然後起身。

「既然如此，只好由我變身，成為兒子的伴侶。」

那天，她帶著久未有的開朗心情回到家，然後對兒子說：

「今天母親找到很適合你的伴侶，所以明天早上你去那山谷對面的岩石上吧，那裡一定有位跟你一樣懷抱寂寞心情的美麗新娘在等待你。而我這個母親呢，在你娶妻之後就沒有用處了，所以我會前往距離這裡好幾座山峰遠的地方。你們兩人要永遠永遠和睦生活喔。」

母親這麼說後，便離開了那個家。兒子感到不可思議，隔日早上，他按照母親的指示，走到山谷對面，那裡有位把臉染黑的（刺青）的美麗女孩盛裝等待。

「啊，您是我的丈夫！」

「啊，您是我的妻子！」

二人緊緊握著手，這是結為永不變心夫婦的盟約。也就是說，身為母親的她，為了騙自己的兒子，於是在自己臉上刺青。星霜荏苒過了幾百年，據說至今他們子孫的高砂族女人，在成為有夫之婦時，一定會在臉上刺青，這樣的習俗即源自這個故事。

無人島的故事

兄妹兩人好不容易漂流到某個孤島的岩石旁，一邊互相把被海水淋濕的衣袖擰乾，一邊靜靜回想剛剛所見的可怕光景。眼看山岳轟然崩塌，火焰沖天，日月無光，人畜悲鳴，與山河震動的巨響合而為

一，在此悽慘時刻，滔滔的洪水吞沒了一切。沉著的兩兄妹，在此激變動盪下，立刻砍倒一棵樹作成木舟，坐上它，一邊漂流在浪濤上，一邊撿拾飄過來的小米穗，把自己的生死交給了天運。不可思議的，他們九死一生，在接近傍晚時漂流到這個小島。於是兩人感謝神明暗中護佑，鬆了一口氣。

「哥哥，這是什麼島？」

因為妹妹出聲詢問，這才回神過來的哥哥，凝神望向四周，但那裡連看似房屋的東西都沒有，除了他們之外，沒有任何人影。

「嗯，望眼所及什麼都沒有，這裡可能是無人島。」

「無人島！無人島！！」

「對啊，這裡一定是無人島。妹妹啊，用不著這樣哭泣。逃離那個可怕世界，漂流到這個島，再怎麼說都是神明暗中保佑。太陽已經下山，四周都暗了，今晚就在這個岩岸上小睡一下吧。」

兩兄妹互相握著手，在寒冷中睡著。醒來後，發現熾盛炫目的太陽已經高高昇起。二人心想這裡或許有人居住，於是到處探看，不過最後徒勞無功。瞭解情形後的哥哥，鼓勵妹妹合力建造小屋，開墾田園，並將先前沒吃完的小米灑下，在這裡開始了簡單的生活。此後送日迎月幾十回，在四顧茫紗的孤島，不是只有妹妹感到寂寞，在某個夜晚，哥哥對妹妹說：

「妹妹，我們是多麼不幸的人啊。失去父母不久後，被那悲慘的歷史之舟帶到這個島嶼，考慮到將來，這寂寥的孤島生活，對我們兩人來說，絕不會是幸福的生活。當兩人年老，感到手腳不便時，誰會照顧我們呢？或是生病死亡的話，誰會悼念我們的靈魂呢？妹妹啊，千萬別驚嚇，我說的話是世上史無前例的。我們兩人結為夫妻，追求幸福與繁榮，我想這或許是可行之道，能報答救助我們的神，不，我是這麼確信……」

　　妹妹聽了哥哥這席令人意外的話，滿臉通紅，身體一動也不動，兩人之間頓時陷入沉默。皎潔月亮不知何時隱入雲間，孤島的夜晚在深沉的海浪聲裡過去了。歲月如流水，過了十多年後，兩人已有十幾個子女。然後這些子女又相互結為夫妻，分灶各自成家，終於形成一個部落。有一天，以鑄鐵為業的一對兄妹正在鑄鐵，但那日不知為何，鐵變成了火粉四處飛散。而以農為業的一對兄妹在搗小米飯時，也碎裂飛出臼外。看到這怪現象的兩對兄妹，擔心禍及自身，把鐵類、穀類家財載入舟中，並向父母兄妹道別：

　　「父親，母親，各位兄妹，被惡魔詛咒的我們，要到天涯海角的遙遠之邦，想想這許多年來已住慣的島，今天是最後一面了。儘管如此，我們會航行到那未曾見過的國度，在那裡開拓新的村落。那裡有繼承父母親溫暖血流的我們兄妹，會感謝生之喜悅。再會吧……」

在南風中揚起船帆，不久後船就駛離了令人懷念的故鄉之島，消失在遙遠的海路上。留在島上的，是高砂族的祖先，離開島的，則是臺灣人的祖先。因此，今日我們高砂族鐵少，他們臺灣人鐵多，這是不足為奇的。老頭目說完後，拿起了杯子。

祭祀夜晚的故事

從前，在某個山村裡，有位非常美麗的少女，名叫 Sawa（サワー）。有一天，她被母親 Bugo（ブゴウ）帶著，和哥哥 Arimoro（アリモロー）一起到山裡的田地除草。不過柔弱的少女 Sawa 筋疲力盡，倦困至極，不知何時在一棵樹下沉沉睡去。不久後她醒來，發現自己不知何時已被安置在一個從未見過、也未聽聞過的大房子裡。她茫茫然，如作夢般好奇環顧四周，那裡有一位魁梧的頭目慢悠悠來到她面前。

「少女啊，從今天起妳就是我們的家人了。好不好？就是要成為我的女兒喔。」

Sawa 聽完後感到恐懼，抽抽搭搭哭了起來。

「少女啊，不用哭成這樣嘛。比起當那個寒酸家庭的女兒，當我這個頭目的女兒不知道要好上多少。妳真是個幸福的人。」

此時 Sawa 首度開口說：

「請問頭目先生，我為什麼來到這裡？」

頭目聽 Sawa 這麼問，原本溫柔的臉色頓時大變，聲音也變得粗暴，他怒氣滿面，紅著臉怒吼：

「這種事情妳用不著知道。嗯，妳想知道的話就告訴妳吧。妳在那樹蔭裡睡覺時，我就這樣把妳抱回來。妳毫不知情，在我懷裡帶著微笑熟睡，而妳的母親與哥哥卻瘋狂般陷入混亂，哈哈哈哈……」

　　事已至此，Sawa 也無可奈何，唯有聽天由命。月日如流水般，送春迎秋了好幾回。如今 Sawa 已是閉月羞花的十八年華，在某個夏夜，有位青年突然造訪她家。Sawa 按當地習俗，取水來到客人面前。這位青年眼睛眨也不眨地盯著她的臉，然後靜靜開口說：

　　「冒昧請問，您的芳名是？」

　　正值含苞待放妙齡的 Sawa，聽到年輕人這麼問，臉上微微浮現如紅葉散開般的羞色。

　　「我叫作 Sawa。」

　　「Sawa！Sawa！」

　　「咦？您聽到我的名字竟然這麼驚訝，是因為……」

　　「妳就是我尋找多年的妹妹啊。」

　　「啊！所以您是我哥哥！我多麼想念您啊，我……」

　　Sawa 講到「我」，就因為過於開心而說不出話來。

　　「Sawa，妳再也不用擔心任何事了，我有個不錯的計謀。」

　　哥哥 Arimoro 在妹妹耳邊悄悄說了一些話，妹妹 Sawa 雖然眼睛泛著淚水，臉上卻露出清朗的笑容。此事發生後經過數日，在某個夜晚，這個部落舉行了盛大的小米祭，部落裡的年輕人們全都出來喝烈酒，他們讓美麗的 Sawa 站在他們中間，並且瘋狂般地跳舞。就在這時候，眼看背後的刺竹，在無風的情況下也搖晃著，竹木頂端站著一位身穿華麗服飾的青年，隨著竹木彎曲而躍進人們中央，他快速抱起那位美女，然後又跳上高空，消失在暗夜裡。眾人被奪走了年輕人歡樂焦點的美女 Sawa，如夢醒般互看彼此反應不及的臉。

　　「喂，剛剛從空中穿著華麗衣服跳下的是什麼？」

　　「我怎麼知道。」

　　「那抱著 Sawa 又跳上高空的神技，根本不是人類辦得到的。」

　　「是啊，那一定是神。」

因此他們收起酒宴，代之以肅穆的祭壇，然後人們跪在祭壇前祈禱。天空閃耀著如灑下金鋼石般的星星，蕃社的夜晚靜靜地深沉了下去……。

附記這些故事繼續挖掘的話還有很多，不過若連載太久，可能會造成讀者諸君的困擾，所以先在此結束〈傳說的高砂族〉。待過完新年之後，再重新構思寫點什麼。

（原刊於《臺灣警察協會雜誌》第91號，1924年12月25日）

Translation

Translator's Introduction

What follows is a series of legends circulating among Taiwanese indigenous people, which were collected and written down by a Japanese police officer (秋澤烏川) in 1924 when Taiwan was under colonial rule. These mythical stories were published in Japanese in *The Magazine of Taiwanese Policemen Association*. As such, the implied readership was more specific than what is intended here. The original version was read by those who understood the Japanese language and were probably also professionals like the author. This might provide valuable insights into the culture of Taiwanese indigenous people, which was of much practical significance in their day-to-day contact with them. In contrast, the English text presented here is to be enjoyed by the general readers around the world. This means that an overly academic approach may actually spoil rather than enhance the pleasure of reading. Therefore, when diverse ways of translating a term, a sentence or even a passage consisting of several sentences come to mind, which happened frequently enough, I usually prefer those which make the whole paragraph appear natural and fluent rather than literal and precise.

Before providing concrete illustrations, however, I have to confess my sins committed in preparing this translated text. It was NOT translated directly from the Japanese manuscript, but indirectly from the Chinese version published together in this booklet. Thus, the accuracy of my translation has to depend, at least in part, on the extent to which the Chinese translation are faithful to the original text. Nevertheless, the criteria for a good translation are not limited to reliability and precision; elegance counts as well. There are even some cases where the literary effect is best captured by sacrificing reliability and precision in the scientific sense.

The most conspicuous type of examples concerns the names of animals and plants. Things are fine if well-known common names are available, such as foxtail millet. When the species can only be identified by its scientific name, I appeal to the common name of an animal or plant similar to it, such as secretary bird, for the obvious reason that the use of scientific name seems awkward in literature. On the other hand, it is possible that the common names chosen by me happen to be associated with distinct myths and symbols in the culture to which the readers belong. Here I can only caution that Taiwanese indigenous people have their own imaginations about the nature and character of the animals and plants around them, which can be readily discerned from the context provided by the legends.

In saying this, I do not claim that reliability and precision are less important. Thus, with regard to the names of places and tribes, I have tried to find the most widely used Romanised names for purposes of identification. The tribes of Tafalong, Puyuma, and Kaliawan, and the valley named Kalala, are cases in point. Where even the Japanese original was directly translated from aboriginal language in terms of its pronunciation and therefore lacks meaning, such as the mountain called Bunohon, I have added its modern name in brackets as " (White Rock)."

Nonetheless, there are terms whose meanings are unclear in the Japanese manuscript in the first place, which are also indicated in the Chinese translation, such as the term papaku. Of course, one can appeal to similar versions of this tale as told by other tribes, or more modern versions of it, and, by comparing their structures, infer that this term means "spinning top". However. Variations of plot and content are common in stories that are told rather than written down. Before ruling out this possibility, this approach is risky. In cases like this, I have done my best to judge the meaning of the term in question by resorting to the context in which it occurs, and directly substituted an ordinary English word ("silk threads" in this case) for the meaningless romanisation. Another kind of instances also supports the observation that sometimes literal translation hinders accurate understanding. In the tale where stone "fences" were set up on vines to capture the tribesmen who chased after the protagonists, I find it easier for the general readers to understand the logic by translating it more plainly as stone "traps".

Perhaps it is true that no translation could rival the original. Moreover, a rich text such as this one, which records ancient legends, by its very nature demands specialised training in a wide range of disciplines. Many of the characters' names already translated from aboriginal language into Japanese may require an anthropologist's insights into their original meanings in order to decipher the deeper patterns of significance underlying the surface of the narration. Understanding the stories is only the first step, however; expressing them in yet another language is still more challenging. It belongs to the talent of a novelist to convey these delicate details not by describing them in notes or forewords but by having them directly shown through the literary language of the translated text themselves.

I majored in philosophy and is currently studying the history of British political thought. That is another way to admit that I have never studied English literature properly, among other specialisms essential to this task of translation. In spite of this, I have strived to make the resulted text do more than preserve the information contained in the original stories. I hope to keep the tone and the taste as well, even if they have already been diminished in being translated into Chinese in the first place. Thus, for example, instead of rendering "time flowed like a current" into "time flies," I choose to let the simile stand as it is such that the cultural association between time and river remains salient, at the price of making it sound a little bit unnatural of English. I have even attempted to translate a four-line lyric into rhymed poetry—any reader with more knowledge of English poetry should rightly laugh at this child's play. But insofar as it succeeds in arousing the vivid experience of jealousy and other related human sentiment in the reader's mind, it has done its job properly.

A casual reader may begin from whichever story that interests him or her the most. Still, if the thematic differences between the five collections of aboriginal legends are pointed out, the principle by which the original author collected his materials can be observed more clearly. This is helpful in directing the reader's attention to the highlighted feature in each story depending on the collection in which it is grouped, even though most of the stories may incorporate various themes which come under the title of other collections as well.

The first collection includes legends most of which are about more ancient mythical events, such as genesis, the discovery of fire, and the beginning of agriculture in the form of slash-and-burn. In the second group of stories, many natural phenomena are given pre-scientific explanations, including celestial bodies and weather conditions. The next set deals mainly with the origins of tribal customs, such as head-hunting and familial/tribal separation. In the fourth collection, women's jealousy occupies the centre stage and, finally, miscellaneous stories are put together in the last group probably because of the original author's intention to end the series abruptly in the fifth instalment.

There are many themes which are universal in the sense that many cultures in the world have their own version in their mythologies: the great flood, incest, the Oedipus complex, metamorphosis, the conquest of the sun(s), etc. What makes Taiwanese indigenous people's version distinctive is the relatively modern nature of some of the stories. These stories probably happened quite recently in history, for at some places there were even appearances of firearms. This is unsurprising if we know that even today in the twenty-first century, it is still common for these tribesmen to linguistically or pictorially record their own life stories, which actually happened, as myths or legends to be handed down to their descendants.

At this point, some impatient readers may justifiably feel that the translator is being too talkative, which is perhaps the sin of those who once studied philosophy in their life. Nevertheless, impatience is welcomed, and particularly helpful in reading literature for pleasure. If the reader finds a story boring, either because the translation is awful or simply because the story fails to interest him or her, please feel free to blame the translator's inability and directly skip to the next one. If a work cannot entertain you, it does you no good even if you make great efforts to finish reading it from cover to cover. Time flows like a current. Perhaps the day will come when the stories can fascinate you, or, more probably, a second edition can find a translator better qualified than me.

Taiwanese Indigenous People in the Legends (I)

Legend is a reflection of the character of a nation, a history told rather than written. A few years ago, I was invited by the publisher of *Taiwan RiRiXinBao* [a daily newspaper] and contributed more than twenty collected legends to that newspaper. However, since they were written in my leisure time after daily work, I have to apologise for their unsystematic and heterogeneous nature. In writing "Taiwanese indigenous People in the Legends" from scratch here, I hope to do my best to select materials and pay attention to details. That these can interest the reader is the honour hoped for by the present author.

1. A Legend from the Ancient Age of the Gods

It was three thousand years ago in the Age of the Gods. In a mountain called Bunohon [White Rock] in the Central Mountain Range, there was a rather huge old tree the name of which remains unknown. One half of the tree was constituted by wood, the other half by stone. Its lush green foliage covered the whole sky so that the world was dark all day long.

In a summer night, this tree metamorphosed into a God, giving birth to all creatures. From its bottom came one on four legs, with its body covered by furs. Also coming from the bottom was another creature having a tumour on its head, which looked like a tree because its body was connected with two branches and two roots. Following this, a creature which came into existence from the top of the tree had a long shape, and always crawled due to its inability to walk. Finally, coming from the top also was a creature which did not stay on the ground because it possessed wings to fly in the sky. These were the ancestors of what were later called the beasts, the human beings, the snakes, and the birds.

Unfortunately, since the world was dark, they could not talk to one another despite living on a single tree. Nevertheless, one day, all four creatures gathered in a cave. The ancestor of human beings, who were to establish dominion over all other creatures, began the discussion."Dear everybody, in the past we fed on wind only. But somehow, I always feel extremely hungry. Don't you have the same feeling?"

The ancestor of beasts, which seemed to have waited for this moment since long ago, echoed passionately, "Of course! If we don't eat anything else, our lives can no longer be sustained. Look at my belly, I'm already starving!"

The third to join this conversation was the gloomy ancestor of snakes. "Certainly! Anything no matter what is good. I can eat a horse now; I want to satisfy my hunger as soon as possible. Hey, you feel the same as I do, right?"

Thus asked, the cute ancestor of birds eventually said, "Yes, I agree with what all of you have said …."

Seeing that everybody was of the same opinion, the ancestor of human beings announced solemnly, "Let all of us begin to taste everything and take that which caters the most to his taste as his source of food henceforth!"

After this announcement, all of them scrambled over the world to taste everything. What we human beings, the beasts, the snakes, and the birds eat nowadays, result from this ancient agreement.

The ancestor of human beings chose foxtail millet and meat. With regard to foxtail millet, a small part of it cooked in a pot sufficed to provide food for four to five people. In addition, one did not need to farm a large piece of land in order to obtain foxtail fillet; two or three square inches of land was enough to feed all people. When one wanted to eat meat, one only needed to call wild boars, remove their furs, cut the furs into pieces, and put them into a pot to cook. A large platter of delicious meat would automatically result from it. In stark contrast to our modern cry of "Give us the bread!", that was truly a paradise!

To ge back to our story, the ancestor of human beings born from the old wooden-stone tree gave birth to many descendants through intercourse between mothers and sons, and between brothers and sisters. Thus, two tribes were formed within just a few years. One day, the two tribes yelled at each other across a river, comparing the size of their population in terms of the loudness of their voice. In the end, the voice of tribe A proved to be louder than that of tribe B to the extent that even the mountains were shaken by their roar.

With complacency tribe A shouted at tribe B,"Look at our prowess! We don't like to live with you together in the same place. We want to move to the plain downhill. In order to distinguish between you and us, you should be tattooed. If you don't like this discrimination, feel free to hunt our heads! We are the majority and won't be scared of you."

The present author thought that racial discrimination is the patent of the United States, but did not imagine that the Taiwanese indigenous people have had this problem since the Age of the Gods. If the Americans hear of this story, they will probably smile because of the fortune to meet people with common understanding. Those who went to the plains are the ancestors of the Taiwanese people now; those who stayed in the mountains are the ancestors of what was fortunately renamed as Takasagozoku [Taiwanese indigenous people] today. In this way, the Age of the Gods came to an end peacefully.

2. A Legend about Obtaining Tinder

In ancient times, the ancestors of Takasagozoku [Taiwanese indigenous people] had not discovered how to start a fire. All food was eaten raw, and there was no light in the night, which was very inconvenient. One day, those who were physically strong in the tribe gathered together to see if there could be a solution, but they could not come up with any good idea in spite of hard thinking. Consequently, they decided to find tinder separately. Some of them went uphill to high mountains, whilst others ventured into deep valleys instead. Although great efforts were made, nobody succeeded. They were very disappointed and camped at the summit of a mountain overnight.

Late at night, a tribesman yelled excitedly, "Look at the fire! Look at the fire!" Hearing this, other people lying on the grass jumped up and looked into the distance at the sea. They found that there was a glittering fiery light.

"Brilliant!" all tribesmen invariably jubilated. However, since it was located in the sea which was far away from the land, nobody dared to go there. Therefore, they sent a bear, which was renowned for its calmness and courage, to reach it. Yet it was a pity that the bear was swept into the sea by huge waves on its way to the fire. The people then dispatched a leopard, which was famous for its ferocity, for the same mission, but it met the same fate. Seeing this, they sighed with despair. At this moment, a muntjac came to them and said, "Everybody here, please send me to obtain the tinder. Even though I was insulted and underrated by other beasts frequently in the past, I will risk my life to accomplish this mission."

After listening to these words full of manhood, the tribesmen decided to dispatch the muntjac to reach the fire. It jumped into the sea like a flying bird, fearlessly and in high spirits. It was not afraid of the mountainous waves coming towards it, keeping itself floating on the surface of the sea. Finally, it succeeded in obtaining the tinder and getting it back. Everybody was very happy.

"Oh! The brave and lovely muntjac!" People expressed their gratefulness to it, caressing its back so that its furs have since then become beautifully smooth and shining. This legend tells us that those who are usually ridiculed yet tolerate it and keep their self-respect, are usually those who can exert great power in a crisis. As such, this legend cannot be simply regarded as a childish fairy tale in ancient ages.

3. A Legend about the Naughty God

What is troublesome in the world? There is nothing which causes more trouble than the Naughty God who can metamorphose into anything at will. Yes, he uses his divine powers to cause trouble to righteous human beings. This is wholly unjust!

Long ago, there was a god called Idotsuku in the heaven. One day, he was so bored that he peeped through the clouds to see the mundane world, observing clearly that human beings were living there.

"This is so interesting. Let me join them as well!" said Idotsuku. Thus, from heaven he landed on the ground recklessly. He came to a tribe called Tafalong and married a beautiful woman named Rume. However, nobody knew what he was thinking when he flied back to the heaven a few days later, and then brought back two sections of bamboo and two silk threads. After that, he no longer farmed on his land, but hid in a room of a dark house, concentrating on twisting the threads. Needless to say, his family was baffled by his behaviour; even his neighbours laughed at his idiocy every time they met him:

"Although he is a god coming from the heaven, he cannot earn a living by twisting threads only, right?"

"As the proverb goes, there is no cure for idiots. This applies so well to Idotsuku!"

"So he is probably exiled by other gods and wanders in the mundane world below. Hahahaha!"

Regardless of these comments, Idotsuku soon produced a silk string more than a thousand fathoms long. He then went uphill alone, drove wooden stakes into the ground everywhere, tied the silk string on the stakes, and tied the end of the string to the foot of the mountain. Incredibly, when he forcefully pulled the string from below, the luxuriant woods were all pulled down with a tremendous noise, as if there had been hundreds of crashes of thunder coming down simultaneously. After the woods withered, Idotsuku set them on fire and burned them down. Finally, he played a spinning top on the resulted wasteland, and threw the unburned remains of the woods towards people's farmland.

"It is really outrageous to throw remains of the woods into other people's farmland. Idotsuku is a god, so he does not understand what it is to be humane," clamoured the owners of the land. However, being afraid of Idotsuku's divine powers, they cannot do anything to him in his presence. So they went uphill secretly during the night, threw the woods back into Idotsuku's farmland, and came back home as if nothing had happened. In the next morning, Idotsuku discovered this, and peed there so that his urine carried the woods down again into people's land. He then immediately planted the seeds of moonflower on his land. At this moment, his father-in-law could not put up with him anymore and said to him, "Idotsuku, I admire your divine powers. But why do you, being so smart, sow the seeds of moonflower? I beg you to sow the seeds of rice or foxtail millet instead!"

"My father! Please wait for a moment and enjoy the pleasure of harvest!" Subsequently, when the moonflowers bloomed luxuriantly, Idotsuku built ten barns. Knowing nothing, his mother-in-law could not tolerate his crazy behaviour and, out of her womanly emotion, hid herself from him. Nonetheless, Idotsuku did not care about this at all. He came to his yard and laid flat a straw mat on the ground. He stood on the mat and shook his own body. His body hair dropped onto the mat and became human beings. He smiled slightly and led these people to harvest the fruits of moonflower. They brought these fruits back home, cutting them open by an indigenous knife. As a result, from each seed in the fruit came four to five litres of foxtail millet, instantaneously piling up to form a small mountain in the yard. All ten barns were now filled with golden foxtail millet.

"Hey, now I'm going to punish those who mocked me," Idotsuku said to himself while walking to the seashore. The people there were distributing what they caught from the sea. Surprisingly, everywhere Idotsuku swaggered past the lively fish became black stones. Everyone was shocked and scared, crying and pulling his sleeves to apologise for what they had done and said to him in the past. Consequently, the black stones were transformed into lively fish again. As the story goes, the black stones that remained then are the charcoal we see now.

One day, on their way from the land to their home, the tribesmen saw some beautiful woods dropped on the ground. They felt happy and brought them back home. When they laid the woods down, the woods metamorphosed into Idotsuku, who said, "Thanks! I lay at the side of the road because I was too tired. Thanks to your help of bringing me here on your shoulder, I am exempted from the tough journey through the paths in the mountain. I am really grateful to you."

Another day, Idotsuku transformed himself into a driftwood log carried by a river to its bank. When a tribesman was going to pick it up, it suddenly metamorphosed into Idotsuku and laughed for a while. On another occasion, he changed his form into a deer running across the people's farmland. After they put down their hoes and chased after him, he sneaked to their back and hid their hoes in the grass, going back home as if nothing had happened. Such were his acts of mischief, which the tribesmen did not know how to deal with.

Nevertheless, on a day of intense lightning and thunder, Idotsuku flied back to the heaven for the third time. Since then, he has never come to the mundane world. The tribesmen are so happy that today they still do not cross the boundaries of other tribes; they do not drop any litter; when foxtail millet is being harvested, they worship their ancestors and Idotsuku and offer them animal sacrifices such as boars and chickens; in addition, when they are catching fish, if someone passes by, they will share some of the caught fish with him; and so forth. The Takasagozoku [Taiwanese indigenous people] is well known for their ferocity and aggressiveness, yet they can do nothing at all with Idotsuku's mischievous behaviour. This is what makes life endlessly interesting!

4. A Legend about the Female-Only Island

On a leisurely day in spring a fisherman unfurled the sails of his bamboo boat and sailed into the outer sea. However, somehow, he could not catch a single fish on that day. He was very frustrated and threw away his fishing rod to the edge of the boat, gazing vacantly at the sea. There floated a small dark island.

"Ah! What a beautiful island! Let me get there and take a break." He immediately sailed towards the island and landed on it recklessly. "This feels so good!" he said to himself, taking out a pack of tobacco from his waist pocket. Surprisingly, all of a sudden, he discovered that the island began to move, and then there was an extremely loud noise coming from below.

"Hey! Who is smoking on my back when I am taking a nap?"

"You scared me! Dear Mr. Island, you can speak like a human being!"

"Hey! Are you kidding me? I am not an island but Mr. Whale. You idiot!" roared the whale, shaking his body angrily so that the fisherman was threw to a kingdom several kilometres away. That was a foreign country he had never seen nor heard of. Besides, he was surrounded by nothing but women, who looked at him curiously and began the following conversation.

"What is this?"

"It seems to have the shape of a human being, but it differs from us in that it is black, and its skeleton and body are larger. Perhaps it is an ominous deformed animal."

"Ah! It is probably the boar which we have heard of in the ancient legends. Let's catch it and feed it in our pigsty."

Listening to these comments, the fisherman was shocked. Although his skin was really black, he was still depressed about being mistaken for a boar, crying with tears rolling down his cheeks. Nevertheless, those women did not care about his weeping and jailed him in a small house, merely providing him with daily leftovers such as the remains of taros. After just a few days, the fisherman, who became thinner and thinner, sneaked to the seashore when the women were asleep. He gazed afar under moonlight and thought of his homeland which he missed so much but to which he could no longer go back. He couldn't help bursting into tears. At this moment the whale he met before emerged leisurely from the sea again. Seeing it, the fisherman put his palms together and begged the whale.

"Mr. Whale, thanks to you, I suffered from such humiliating hardship. I beg you to bring me back to my homeland!"

"My poor fisherman! Sit on my back! I will bring you back immediately."

The fisherman followed the whale's instructions and jumped onto its back. Then the whale swung its tail just a few times, and the homeland which he had been missing so much appeared instantaneously before him.

"Ah! I see the land! I see the forest of my homeland!" the fisherman yelled with delight. The whale told him, "Hey, Mr. Human Being, please give me some sacrifice after you get back home!"

"You are my rescuer. I know what to do."

"This is your promise!"

After a loud ding-dong, he was thrown back to the land. He immediately returned home with ecstasy, held the hands of his wife and children, and wept with happiness.

"Ah! My husband, we worried so much about you, and we are very pleased to see you come back home!"

"I'm sorry to make you worry about me. I was brought to the terrible Female-Only Island by a whale."

"The Female-Only Island!"

"Do not misunderstand it! Although it was an island where only women lived, I was mistaken for a boar there, and was forced to eat only leftovers and the remains of taros."

"They went so far as to regard my husband, so important to me, as a boar …."

"Don't be angry! It is exactly because I was considered as a boar that I could come back."

His wife experienced intense jealousy when she heard of the "Female-Only Island," got angry after being informed that the fisherman was taken as a boar, but finally smiled because of his husband's words.

"I am very happy! To me, you are my dear husband; to our children, you are the important father. Such a man finally comes back and remains intact." She fell into her own delight, turning around and around cheerfully.

"Ah! There's no time to waste. I made a promise to Mr. Whale…."

Then the fisherman returned to the seashore, laid a grass mat on the ground, placed wine, pies, and betel nuts on it, and waited for the whale. After a while, no sooner had the whale appeared vaguely in the waves far away than the huge waves swept away the sacrifices into the sea, leaving only the grass mat at the seashore. The rhythm of the waves along the coastline today results from this. In addition, legend has it that the beautiful bridge connecting the main island of Taiwan with the Green Island fell apart into the sea at this moment so that the two islands have since then become separated and isolated.

*Originally published in *The Magazine of Taiwanese Policemen Association*, no. 87 (25 August 1924).

Taiwanese Indigenous People in the Legends (II)

1. A Legend about the Conquest of a Sun

People living in the frigid and the temperate zones are afraid of coldness, so they highly revere the glowing sun full of heat and fervour, regarding it as the king of the gods, and regarding the moon, which illuminates the night, as subordinate to him. In contrast, those living in the tropics and the subtropics dislike the torrid summer, and thereby venerate the bright and clear moonlight at night, deifying it as the lord god, and relegating the sun to a lower rank. Those living in regions of extremely high temperature are even hostile to the sun. The legend to be told here originates from such a region.

In ancient times there were two suns irradiating the whole world both day and night. As a result, the rivers dried up, the farmlands became barren, and there was a shortage of food. The poor people were helpless and about to starve to death. It is common at all times and in all places that people rely upon gods in desperate situations. Unfortunately, although they prayed to the god for help, nothing effective had happened.

"The god should save us from this miserable plight! All of us prayed piously together, yet he did not respond to us. He is so merciless ..." a tribesman in the crowd shouted with a feverous tone, and other people yelled agitatinglyto echo his cry.

"That's true. We should no longer depend upon such a god without mercy. We should resolve our problems on our own."

"Wake up, my compatriots! Rise up, everybody!"

People's emotions came to a climax, and the atmosphere was filled with violent fury. At this moment, two young men elbowed their way forwards through the crowd and announced, "Dear everybody, please don't worry. We two will set out to shoot the sun to death. We hope you can put up with the temporary sufferings and wait for the day to come when today's sorrow and anger turn into joy and delight."

After saying this, these two youngsters, with their foxtail millet and pomelos, bravely began their journey to conquer the sun. In the long and arduous trek extending several decades, they put up with the toil, overcame the difficulties, and finally arrived at the boundary of the world. Their morale was high, their mind fearless. Standing on the edge of a cliff, they nocked their arrows and pulled back their bows, eagerly waiting for the sunrise. After a while, the vividly red sun rose over the sea in the distance, shining brightly like melting steel. The courageous young men seized this opportunity and immediately shot their arrows, which accurately stuck into the centre of the sun. The scene was tragic and miserable. A large amount of blood poured down like a torrent, producing red waves on the sea. It was a pity that one of the youngsters was swept away into the sea by the sun's blood and died. The other one, who fortunately survived, did not feel any delight after shooting down the sun. Grieving the loss of his companion, he quietly set out for home with loneliness. The seeds of pomelos which the youngsters threw away during their journey of conquest had now become huge trees bearing a lot of fruits. The surviving youngster took them as sorrowful memories of his dead friend, and finally went back to the homeland by following them as signposts. His parents, who saw him off when he set out to conquer the sun, had already deceased. The old man who greeted him at the door was his friend. Besides this surprise, the youngster was touched by the scenes when his parents were still alive.

"Let us welcome our saviour!"

"Thanks to this benefactor, we are given the night and the coolness. Without the night, life could not be happy; without the coolness, the crops could not bear fruits."

"Certainly! Let this honourable feat be eulogised forever!"

Under bright and clear moonlight, the tribesmen drank a toast to one another with joy and gratefulness. An old man stood on the podium, gazed at the sky, and said, "Dear everybody! Do you know of the moon and the stars glowing above our heads? In the past when there were two suns and no night, what shone in the sky were only the suns which made us suffer. However, this courageous young man shot down one of them, the blood of which poured everywhere and became the moon and the stars hanging in the sky. Tonight, thanks to this youngster, we can enjoy the bright and clear moonlight and the beauty of the constellations."

Outbreak of applause followed like crashes of thunder. Under the shadow of fragrant trees, in the continuous breeze, the ecstatic people forgot that it was late in the night, and drank continually to celebrate this legend.

2. A Legend about the Sun, the Moon, and the Star

A father felled a huge old Formosan cypress in which, according to legend, a tree spirit dwelled. After relaxing for a while, he said to his sons who were busy transporting the wood, "My raging thirst does not seem to be quenched. Bring me some water from the bank of the stream."

The sons obeyed their father's order and went to the valley of the stream with bamboo buckets. However, on that day the stream, in which transparent water usually flowed slowly, was opaque and muddy despite the absence of rainfall. Surprised as they were, they did not inquire into the causes of the turbid water. So, they returned empty-handed to tell their father what they saw. The father said nothing but laughed helplessly. A moment later the sun set, and the day was over. The next day, the sons followed their father's command again and arrived at the streambank; the water was still muddy as the day before. Another day passed, and when they went there for the third time, the water become even more turbid. After listening to his sons' report, the father frowned and then said calmly, "This must be caused by someone who played some tricks upstream. Is it an ox, a boar, or a human being? Go there and behead him mercilessly!"

The sons set out for the valley of the stream high-spiritedly, searched upstream, and, as their father had conjectured, found a man who was bending his head between his butts and making the stream water dirty. Seeing this, they knocked him down when he was absent-minded and beheaded him with fury. Nevertheless, when they looked at the head meticulously, how could this be, it was the head of their father, who had assigned them such a task! After figuring out the situation, the sons were surprised to the extent of madness and sighed with grief. But what had happened could not be changed. They went back home crying and informed their mother of what they had done. The mother said, "Since you have the courage to hunt your father's head, it should be easy for you to hunt those of other people. Go forward! Hunt their heads immediately! You are not allowed to come back home before collecting several hundreds of heads!"

The mother drove her sons away from home angrily and rudely. The sons bowed their heads with tears. Then the younger of the two sons touched his elder brother's shoulder and said, "As such, we have to obey what our mother has said and hunt as many heads as possible. At least we must make the soul of our dear dead father rest in peace and accomplish what our mother has asked us to do as compensation. I've heard that the tribesmen of Puyuma are renowned for their ferocity. Once they catch sight of their enemies, they will chase after them no matter how far away till the boundaries of the sky and the sea. We can take advantage of their character and lure them into Kalala Valley, where we set up stone traps so as to hunt dozens of heads all at once!"

"Oh, my younger brother! Your idea is really good. Let's begin our conquest now!" So, the brothers killed a leopard in a dark valley deep in the mountain and went to the tribe of Puyuma with its blood. After checking that the children of the tribe were asleep, the brothers shot them with guns and hit three of them. Other adult tribesmen were suddenly awakened by the sound of the unexpected gunshot. They found the brothers in no time and chased after them with firearms. The brothers thought that the plan would be successful, so they dropped the leopard blood along the path of escape, pretending that they were wounded in order to tempt the tribesmen to follow them. At the same time, both sides of the stream saw vines paved like a bridge, with huge stones installed upon them in advance. The brothers then cut down all the vines simultaneously, and in loud noises of the stones they killed dozens of tribesmen chasing after them at once. They brought the heads of these tribesmen back home as sacrifices, worshipping the soul of their dead father and atoning for their sin before their mother. After that, they danced with their younger sister before the alter.

As a result, surprisingly, the brothers' and the sister's feet sank below the surface of the ground, followed by their lower legs and then even their waists. In this way, their bodies gradually sank into the ground. When their heads were about to submerge, they spoke together to their mother,

"As we wished, we worship the soul of our dead father and give consolation to our mother, with no other last words remaining to say. So let us sing and dance like this, sinking below the surface of the ground. The moon which will rise to the summit tonight is the elder brother; the sun which will rise from the east to the sky is the younger brother (it should not be neglected that, like "A Legend about the Conquest of the Sun," the sun here is subordinated to the moon, too); and the large stars which will shine through the sky in darkness is the sister. Dear mother, we pray that you will be healthy and happy forever …."

So the three sang while submerging into the ground. In the winter, the sun sets earlier; in the evening fog, from the mountains in the east, rises the bright and clear moon; a moment later, the gently-glowing stars begin to twinkle; after that, when the cocks crow at dawn, the sun rises from the east to the sky again… . Legend has it that in this way the elder brother, aka the moon, and the younger brother, aka the sun, approach and greet each other once a month. This unending process will recur everlastingly.

3. A Legend about Thunder and Lightning

Once upon a time, a couple with their son lived amicably in a mountain village. One day, the father and the son went out hunting early, but they did not return in the evening. In the dim light of the fire, the mother worried about them. Were they devoured by a terrible monster? Or did they fall into a deep stream? With typical women's emotion, she was anxious about her husband and son. At night, the son came back alone silently.

"Ah! You're finally back. I worried about you so much. Come, get upstairs now! Huh? Where is your father …?"

When he was queried the whereabouts of his father, the son burst into tears. "Both of us lost our way. Subsequently I could not find my father, and then made great efforts to get back here alone."

"What? You left your father alone in the mountain and came back yourself? You the son of filial impiety! Even though you could not see your father, at least you could call his name and maybe he would respond …."

"No. There was no response from my father after I called his name several times."

Hearing this, the mother became furious. She lit a torch and rushed into the night fog to search for her husband. Finally she found him in the valley of a stream, embracing him with ecstasy. "Ah! It's so nice that you are still alive! Your son is really filially impious!"

Back at home, after listening to his wife's report, the father scolded his son, "You son of filial impiety! You said that you had called my name and I did not respond. How could the voice of mine, your father, not be transmitted to your ears? The sound passed through the whole mountain! You called my name so loudly that it was impossible I, your father, did not respond. Hear this voice! Hear this voice!"

After roaring in this way, the father held the mother's hands and then went to the heaven. After that, the father became the thunder, and the mother the lightning. That is to say, the father's voice then was the crash of thunder, and the mother's torch was the flash of lightning. This legend is still being handed down today.

4. A Legend about the King of Birds Lifting the Sky

At the time of Takasagozoku's (Taiwanese indigenous people) ancestors, the sky was not far away from the ground. As a result, people could not get to the ground; instead, they dug underground caves and took them as their dwelling place. Because this was extremely inconvenient and caused much suffering, one day they convened a meeting in order to live happily on the vast ground regardless of any means. However, nobody was willing to accept the mission, with long sighs being let out in the meeting. Finally, a young man sitting at the rear went forward and said, "If we want to remove the tormenting heat of the sun, there is no other way than to lift the sky up. We human beings and the beasts living on the ground are of no use at all for this purpose. The only one who can fulfil this important responsibility are the birds flying in the sky. Nothing else can do this work. I hope we can gather all birds together and come up with a better solution in detail."

Other people could not help but cheer and applaud the wit of this youngster. Then the chieftain yelled loudly towards the sky, "All birds over the world! Come here immediately to take part in what we are planning now!"

After hearing this voice, the birds were curious about what had happened and scrambled to the people. Then the chieftain told them seriously, "Dear birds! As you have seen, the sky is very close to the ground so that the burning deaths caused by the sun every day are countless. Thus, we dug holes below the ground and have been living there. We belive you would not like to live with such inconvenience and suffering either. That is, if the sky is moved to a higher position, you can fly among the clouds at will, and we can also walk on the ground anywhere as we see fit. For the benefit of both you and us, please lift the sky higher up so that all of us can be liberated from the hardship of such torridity!"

The first who came in front of the people was the hawk. "This is just a piece of cake. All I need to do is to flap my wings in the sky for two or three times, and the sky will be blown away to a higher place," said the hawk with arrogance. However, the sky did not panic at all after the hawk flied towards it and flapped his wings. Consequently, the hawk flied back, scratching his head.

The next who appeared before the people was the crow. "Hahahaha!

Dear everybody, look at the embarrassment of the hawk who cannot fulfil his promise! I used to lived in the sun so that my body has become so black. Such is the good relationship between the sun and me. So, let me visit him and negotiate with him." The crow then flied to the sun but did not return after a long time.

"The crow can't do it, either!" the people sighed with sorrow on their faces. The youngster who recommended this idea also betrayed uneasiness, looking around at the birds present there. Finally, there came a tiny bird called Tatachiyu with small steps. Seeing this, other birds pulled one another's sleeves …, no, it's their wings, and laughed at him.

"Look at him! There is no cure for idiocy. How dare the stupid mini Tatachiyu be so cheeky and go forward!"

"Tatachiyu does not really understand his own limits. He is shameless and knows not what other birds think about him. Yet I also pity him. Even the brave and ferocious hawk ended in failure, and the crow who was in very good relationship with the sun has not returned intact …."

Tatachiyu did not take other birds' derision seriously and, with his lovely tiny body, he used up all its strength and warbled, "Tachiuka, tachiuka, tachiuka …." The sound was resounding, clear, and sonorous so that the people could not help being enchanted. The sound then gradually spread to all directions. As a consequence, the sky was moved by it and rose upwards rapidly.

Thanks to this tiny bird, we can live on the ground peacefully now. Therefore, Tatachiyu has become the king of the birds and, after millenniums, is today deified as the highly-esteemed holy bird.

5. A Legend about the Wind, the Rain, and the Snow

One day the Wind, the Rain, and the Snow gathered together, each of whom boasted about his own powers.

"In this world, there is nobody who is as powerful as I am. No matter where I go, there is nothing which is not moved by me." The first one who arrogantly said this with his nose in the air is the Wind. After him, the Rain followed immediately, "I am not as rude as Mr. Wind. Yet I do possess the power to infiltrate the soil gradually so that even a huge mountain can collapse. In comparison with us, Mr. Snow has only a womanly white face. He can't do anything!"

"Certainly. Mr. Snow as a friend of ours is really too weak. Hahahaha ...," the Wind echoed. Having listened to the Rain's and the Wind's derision calmly, the Snow spoke for the first time at this moment. "It is true that my body is as white as a woman, that I am not uncatchable like Mr. Wind, and that I am not humid and sombre like Mr. Rain. Nevertheless, wherever I go, everything in the world becomes silver in colour. The biting coldness must be chilling to the bone. In my opinion, your powers are nothing but small tricks."

After hearing this, the Wind and the Rain were furious and red in the face. "That's fine! Let us actually compare our powers with one another then!" No sooner had the Wind said this impatiently than he employed all his strength to blow. As a result, the heaven and the earth were shaken, the stones blown away, the trees knocked down, and the clouds were moving like a rapid steam. This was an astonishing and scaring scene. "Hey! Look at what I have done! What great powers of mine! Hahahaha …. Mr. Rain, show off your powers as well to make the Snow fearful!"

The Rain replied positively and poured down heavy rain. The rivers and the valleys surged in no time, and the muddy current stormed downstream like a waterfall. "Hehehehe, Mr. Rain's ability is really respectable," applauded the Wind with such annoying remarks.

The Snow looked at them and smiled. Now it was his turn. He silently and calmly sprinkled the snow like white feathers. Consequently, the lush green grass and woods immediately withered. In both the fields and the mountains in sight, there was nowhere that was not covered by whiteness. The water was frozen, the crops chilled, and the people's bodies became cold. The people had hiden themselves in caves, laughing at the haughtiness of the Wind and the Rain. Now they were trembling with fear and coldness, kneeling down before the Snow. Seeing this, the Wind and the Rain lost their morale and disappeared stealthily.

That the Takasagozoku (Taiwanese indigenous people), who live in the mountains of high altitudes and know no fear of the wind and the rain, are so afraid of coldness, can be observed from this small legend.

*Originally published in *The Magazine of Taiwanese Policemen Association*, no. 88 (25 September 1924).

Taiwanese Indigenous People in the Legends (III)

1. A Legend about the Origin of Head Hunting

When the Emperor of Japan is in power, his influence shines over everything in the world. It is praiseworthy that even the weeds in the deep mountains of the isolated southern island can benefit from his grace. Three thousand years ago, a god named Nibunu landed at Mount Jade and created human beings for the first time. Because they were created by the god personally, the people then were very innocent and were allowed to enjoy a longevity which almost amounted to immortality without aging. Therefore, even if one lost his life by accident, he could be resurrected by Nibunu's divine powers. However, after thus bothering the god five times, he would be regarded as no longer being of any use to this world and will consequently be abandoned. The reason might be that, even if the deaths were accidental, he who died consecutively for more than five times was considered by the god as not cherishing his own life and should thus be deserted.

Back to our topic, one day Nibunu left a man who had died for the second time in his dwelling and went out to deal with some more urgent matters. Afterwards, another god called Soesoha, who was very nosy, came to Nibunu's dwelling and held the dead man, crying mournfully and continuously. Then he dug a hole in the dwelling, buried the corpse therein, covered it with earth, and fell to the ground weeping. After the urgent matters had been over, Nibunu returned to his dwelling and was surprised by the scene. Nonetheless, since Soesoha had already cried, Nibunu could not do anything with it. Since then, it has become customary that people bury the dead in their home and cry over it. This custom has never been changed for three millenniums.

From then on, people had the honour to be able to die suddenly no matter when. Nevertheless, the human beings' astonishing power of reproduction still shoddily produced many that were of poor quality. Therefore, in order to rid the world of these bastards, Nibunu called the great flood and made everywhere full of muddy water. As a result, the hills were submerged by the dirty water in no time. The people made huge efforts to flee and gathered on the summit of Mount Jade again.

"What a formidable flood!"

"Everywhere I can see is ran over by dirty streams. Isn't this pleasant?"

"Hey! Hey! Don't rattle on there! You will offend the god!"

Since that time, there has been such a cynical type who likes to gag, and such a kind who regards the god as omnipotent and thus acts neurotically.

"I feel hungry!" said a man as if he had suddenly hit upon this idea. Other people held their belly and echoed, "So hungry!" There was no cereal at that time. The people fed on the beasts hunted by them. As such, in the predicament of the great flood, they could not find food. Thus, a strong man killed the dog he reared. Seeing this, the man who gagged just a moment ago pierced the head of the dog with a bamboo pole, brandished it, and walked among the people. Although some frowned upon this, many found it very interesting and applauded cheerfully.

"Look at the dog head on the bamboo pole!"

"Though it is only a head, it still opens its eyes properly!"

"Without the body, it is unexpectedly intriguing and fascinating!"

After hearing other people's remarks, the gagging man became ever more complacent. This time he killed a monkey and substituted its head with that of the dog. People were more and more interested and praised his novelty.

"The head of a monkey alone can be so interesting. It would be far funnier if it were the head of us human beings!"

"Humph! If the guys who were arrogant and domineering in the past were suddenly dead, it would be so exhilarating to dry their pale heads on the top of bamboo poles!"

"Amusing! Amusing!"

Having become murderous, the crowd took the life of the wicked child who was loathed in the tribe, pierced his head on the top of a bamboo pole, and danced enchantedly with ecstasy. This head-hunting dance might have catered to the god's will so that the flood immediately receded, and the hills and the wilderness came into sight again.

"The water has receded. Let's go to a fertile land! Then let's organise a team to hunt and collect the heads of people in other tribes. If the heads of our tribesmen alone can be so interesting, how pleasant it will be to hunt the heads of our enemies?" Everybody held weapons in their hands, stormed towards the clouds and fogs in the dawn, and left Mount Jade.

2. A Legend about the Origin of Splitting Families

Once upon a time, there was a young hunter full of filial piety called Tomaikoru. He went uphill hunting even in windy mornings or rainy evenings. Besides, he also farmed in the field and persented the harvested crops to his father, which he regarded as the utmost pleasure. One day, he carried his firearms as usual and went out in the starlight. In that morning, the heavy fog surrounded the mountain paths like a cloud. He walked in the mountain and panted, inhaling the fog and sneezing involuntarily. Following this, there was another man who similarly sneezed in the fog.

"What? There should be no other people than I in this mountain. The sneeze just a moment ago was so strange!" said Tomaikoru to himself, looking around but failing to find anyone.

"So strange!" at this moment came the same words from the fog. He followed this voice to find the speaker and subsequently found a luxuriantly blooming crepe flower there. Tomaikoru came in front of the flower, gazed at it for a while, and said, "It is you who imitated my speech a moment ago!"

As a consequence, the crepe flower responded with the same words, "It is you who imitated my speech a moment ago!" Hearing this, the hunter replied, "What on earth do you want to do by continually imitating human speech?" He drew out his waist sabre before finishing his utterance. However, a voice came from the flowers scattering on the ground one after another, "Wait a moment …. Dear young man, please do not hurt me even if you want to cut down the tree."

Until now he had not discovered a human being hidden in the tree.

He then felled the tree from its bottom, and a beautiful woman appeared from the breach as expected.

"What? Why are you here?" Tomaikoru felt astonished. The beautiful woman smiled and said, "I am the spirit of this crepe flower. I have always hoped to come to this world, yet no matter how I tried, I have never been able to leave this tree. Thanks to you, my wish is finally fulfilled today. There is nothing more delightful than this. In order to repay your kindness, I would like to be your ..., no, please allow me to be your wife."

Thus, under the tree where the crepe flowers fell all over the ground, they married and built a simple grass hut. However, the filially pious Tomaikoru did not forget his father despite having been falling in love. Whether in the morning or in the evening, every day he went from this hut, through a brook, back to his father's home, farmed in the field there till night, and then came back to the hut where his wife waited for him. Seeing this, the father sympathised with his son. One day he called his son to him and said, "Dear Tomaikoru, I understand very well your meticulous filial piety. But you no longer need to come back home every day like before. It has been raining heavily recently, so the brook will surge very rapidly. No matter what you say, this is just too dangerous. Therefore, from now on, only when you hunt a deer in the mountains do you need to come here and bring its head with you. That you and your wife can love and cherish each other and live together forever is the most filially pious deed for me as your father."

From then on, whenever Tomaikoru caught a deer, he visited his father and spent that day in his father's home. Time passed like flowing water. Now Tomaikoru had been aged and had difficulties even in crossing a brook. Thus, his father gave him a figurine and ordered him to worship the god with the sacrifice of beast skulls every time he went out hunting. Consequently, the father and the son were totally separated and became two independent families, passing the rest of their lives peacefully. Legend has it that the commencement of family separation in Takasagozoku (Taiwanese indigenous people) originates from this story.

3. A Legend about a Canoe

Since ancient times, the Sun Moon Lake has been filled with green water. Today there is a canoe floating on it, which has become the central problem to be resolved in Taiwan Power Joint-Stock Company's construction work. About this canoe there is a legend.

Once upon a time, there were five young men who had good relationship with one another. One day, they went hunting together deep into the Central Mountain Range, yet, somehow, they did not encounter any prey on that day. The sun was about to set to the west mercilessly with purple haze surrounding the mountains. They were exhausted and sat on a huge rock, gazing at the scene of sunset absent-mindedly. No words were uttered, as if they had been assimilated into the silence of the deep mountains. At this moment, a white deer ran past them as rapidly as an electric spark. Nobody knew whence this deer came. The five young men had been motionless, but after seeing this they immediately set out to catch it. The white deer finally ran to the Sun Moon Lake and jumped into the water like a flying bird. It floated on the surface and swam to an island in the lake. The young men stood by the lakeside, looking vacantly at the water surface as if they had been dreaming. Surprisingly, there appeared a rat sitting on a floating wood chip of a camphor tree. The young men saw him and finally uttered some words for the first time, "Hey! Hey! Dear Mr. Rat on the water, how do you sit on a tiny wood chip without submerging? How do you go forward?"

The rat heard the voices of the young men and turned his head glaring at them. But it remained silent from beginning to end, paddling forwards by using its tail as a rudder.

"This is really incredible!"

"What on earth should we do in order to float on such a deep water?"

"The depth of this lake is several hundred meters. How can we cross it?"

"That's unusual. It is a god. Don't doubt it at any cost!"

"Yes. Let us follow that god's revelation and cross this lake!"

Thus the young men felled a large tree and built a wooden canoe therefrom, where a plank was trimmed to make a rudder. They let it float on the surface of the lake under sunlight at dusk, and it wobbled peacefully with small waves. Then they excitedly jumped into the canoe. To them, who had been accustomed to go up and down barefoot in the mountains, this brisk feeling was a pleasure which they had never experienced before. The young men paddled towards the island quickly in high spirits, just like children. They consequently caught the white deer which had just fled, and then returned to the lakeside. A tribesman saw all this stealthily from a gap between trees and, after the young men disembarked, ran to them and said, "This tool is so convenient. Would you please give it to me?"

"Hey! What's wrong with you talking to us so loudly?"

"Ah! My apologies! In fact, I think that it is not possible at all for you to cross that high mountain back home while bringing such a thing with you. So here is some meat of high quality I bring for you. Come! Let me exchange this for your canoe."

"Hey! Hey! Don't take us as fools. How could that kind of ungenerous meat be exchanged for this canoe? We are not that stupid. Ah! What a pleasure of sitting in a canoe! We are going home by sitting in it." While saying this, the young men pulled the canoe to the land and jumped into it in no time. However, this time the canoe did not feel light at all and gave no comfortable experience. They desperately paddled with their arms, but the canoe did not move an inch. The young men looked at one another, whose facial expression betrayed that they were on the edge of bursting into tears. Seeing this, the tribesman made sarcastic comments, "Humph! I am going to leave for home. Cross that high mountain back to your home by sitting in it then!"

The young men scratched their heads and exchanged their canoe for the meat. The canoe then disappeared in the woods at twilight. Today, the canoe, full of poetic character, still floats on the blue water. When the construction work of the hydroelectric power station is completed, the canoe will probably disappear in the end without leaving any traces.

4. A Legend about a Prophet

Kasautamo became weaker and weaker, feeling that there was not much time left in his life. Thus, he got up from his sickbed and knelt before his parents, saying, "Dear father and mother, thank you for your care during these years. In the end I cannot get well and continue to serve you. As your child, there is nothing more filially impious than this. But I will never abandon my parents in this way. If I stop breathing and my body becomes ice-cold, I will definitely revive to serve you so long as the thumb of my right hand can still move. In case there is no movement of my finger, you can then think of me as having been dead forever ...."

After saying this, he closed his eyes calmly and stopped breathing as if he had fallen asleep. Nevertheless, his thumb still incredibly moved in a slight way. Although his parents were overcome with deep grief, at least they had the anticipation that their son would revive; they therefore took great care of his corpse. From the first day of his death to the morning of the third day, the movement of the finger became gradually slighter. Nonetheless, in the afternoon, it grew faster. In the evening of the fifth day, he began to breathe slightly again and after a while awakened with a smile. His parents and brothers were extremely surprised, and all the people surrounded him celebrating his resurrection.

"Dear father, mother, and my brothers, five days ago I stopped breathing and came to death. A god landed from the heaven, called my name, and held my hands. I was thus brought to the heaven. For the first time I saw the beauty and wonder of the heaven which was beyond words. The gods living in the shiny palace were so elegant. The fairy maidens danced vibrantly in golden robes, which was so alluring. This paradise was beyond the imagination of us living in this mundane world!"

"My goodness! You had been living with the gods?"

"Dear mother, please feel happy for me. I enjoyed five days which were like a dream."

"You had probably lived delightfully. But since you stopped breathing, we had been so worried about you!"

"Dear father, please rest assured. To compensate for this, I have been allowed to possess magical powers which people in the mundane world could not envisage even in their dreams."

"Magical powers! Magical powers!"

"Dear brothers, please listen to me calmly. In the magnificent palace I have just talked about, an eye-catching and especially serious god called me to him and said, 'Become the prophet of human beings! Now I impart the necessary magical powers to you.' Then he personally taught me those magical powers. Afterwards I left the heaven reluctantly and came back to this mundane world."

All the people found this unbelievable and wanted to see such magical powers performed before their eyes. But Kasautamo replied, "The magical powers are revealed by the gods and as such cannot be performed out of no reason," and refused to cast the spells arbitrarily. Nevertheless, after this event he prognosticated many future phenomena in the mundane world and saved people from disasters. Whether predicting the success or failure of a hunting journey and the amount of prey, foretelling the richness or poverty of a yearly harvest, or forecasting the whereabouts of a missing tribesman, every time his prophecy proved to be precise and true.

This Kasautamo was the ancestor of prophets. The Takasagozoku (Taiwanese indigenous people) believe that prophesising is a magical power which belongs to the gods.

*Originally published in *The Magazine of Taiwanese Policemen Association*, no. 89 (25 October 1924).

Taiwanese Indigenous People in the Legends (IV)

1. A Legend about the Two Gods Who Metamorphosed into Cranes

Once upon a time, there were a god and a goddess in the heaven, named Madabira and Risun respectively. One day they landed at a summit in the south and gave birth to four boys and two girls. When Risun was conceiving her second daughter, a dazzling light shone in her belly so that the daughter's body became transparent like a crystal. After ten months a goddess more beautiful than a flower was born, which indeed echoed the above miracle. Her parents especially spoiled their second daughter and brought her up. Time passed like a current, and now came the eighteenth spring in her life. One day, when she went to a valley alone to fetch water as usual, there surprisingly stood a handsome young man whom she had never seen before. Seeing this, she wanted to run away, but the young man came forward and grabbed her by the sleeve, saying, "I am absolutely not a strange man. In fact, I was dispatched by the god of the sea to welcome you. If I put it in this way, you may not understand what happened. To be frank, the god of the sea deeply hopes to marry you and let you live in his harem. Five days later, I will come back again to receive you. Please be prepared and wait for me."

The handsome young man disappeared immediately after he finished his words. Still naïve and innocent, the goddess told her parents every detail of this. They were extremely astonished and made a wooden box at once to confine their daughter therein, sealing it very tightly. However, the light which came from her body shone through the wooden box and leaked out. Even though a second, and then a third, level of wooden box were added, her beauty could still be seen in its totality. Consequently, her parents dug an underground hole and buried her, yet the dazzling light still shone on the ground like a crystal. Her parents sat on it and guarded her day and night. Nothing strange had happened until the evening of the fifth day. Therefore, her parents and brothers felt relieved, and two of her brothers went to the yard to begin mashing foxtail millet.

As a result, the whole sky in the evening reverberated with the sound made by the mortar and pestle. All of a sudden, dark clouds densely covered the sky, the trees were bent by the wind, and huge waves surged like a mountain in no time. Both houses and people were submerged by the muddy current. Fortunately, the whole family fled to the mountain. However, among the children, the beloved second daughter was not seen from beginning to end. Her parents madly called the name of their daughter and gazed at the sea in the distance, seeing clearly that she was being taken away by the god of the sea. Her parents and brothers yelled loudly. She seemed to hear their voice and turned her head, gazing at the mountain in the distance and saying, "Dear father, mother, and brothers, I have realised that all of this is my fate. No matter how sorrowfully I weep now, I cannot escape from the god of the sea. There will no longer be the happy days which I used to share with dear father, mother, and my brothers. However, everything is fate. Please don't cry for me anymore and take this as commemoration."

After saying these words, she cut off her wrist and threw it into the sea. Consequently, the wrist became a fish and swam into the waves. "Dear father, mother, and brothers, after I arrive at where the god of the sea lives, I have to crush foxtail millet every day. The sound of my crushing foxtail millet will ascend to the sky and become thunder. From now on, if you see lightning in the sky and hear crashes of thunder, please take it as my mashing foxtail millet alone."

Her beautiful silhouette thus submerged deeply into the sea. The whole family cried madly while waiting for the water to recede. Nonetheless, the muddy current became ever more turbulent. Therefore, they set out to cross mountains, hoping to find a land full of foxtail millet which had never been discovered before. The brothers felt exhausted and stayed somewhere on their way. But the parents still crossed the mountains in the north and finally arrived at a lowland. They put their feet into the marsh, gazing at the dark blue sea into which the silhouette of their daughter submerged. Surprisingly, wings grew out of their bodies so that they unconsciously metamorphosed into pretty cranes, soaring high into the sky.

Therefore, legend has it that we have never seen a crane being alone. Whenever they appear, they always fly together in pairs, which is an auspicious scene.

2. A Legend about the Maiden Who Rose to the Moon

Once upon a time, in the Kaliawan tribe there was a pretty girl. She had been reared by her stepmother since young. Like an eternal law of the universe, there was not a single day which she did not spend in tears. One day, in the seventeenth spring of her life, her friends invited her to collect shells at the seaside. On their way there, it smelled continuously, which was unbearable. Her friends teased, "Who has farted?" When they arrived at the seaside, the sun had already risen high. They waited for the tide to ebb, opening the bento boxes which they brought with them. To their surprise, despite the beautiful exterior of her bento box, it was full of human excrement inside. Seeing this, her friends laughed out loud.

"The intolerable odour on our way here turns out to be stool!"

"Even I could not have the honour to eat faeces!"

"It doesn't matter to eat excrement! It is in everyone's belly, hahahaha …".

Derided by her friends, she was red-faced and burst into tears. Her friends, however, were unintentional and felt sorry about their poor friend, blaming themselves for being unsympathetic a moment ago. This sentiment turned into merciful tears.

"What a despicable woman!"

"That's true. Even if she is mean-spirited, she should not go too far."

"Let us revenge!"

She had been weeping silently until she interrupted her friends' conversation, "Dear everybody, thank you for your compassion. However, this is not the fault of my stepmother, but mine. If I were not at home, my stepmother would certainly become a kind-hearted woman. Yes, I am going to rise to the heaven now and live peacefully forever. My friends, look at the moon in the night five days later! If you see a girl stretching her legs, putting a cage aside, and taking a rest serenely, then take her as me. Today I will wait on this rock to rise to the moon. Good bye everybody!"

Her friends understood her feelings and therefore did not stop her. They bid her farewell with tears in their eyes and left. The next day, her father heard of this matter and madly came to the seaside, searching everywhere for his lovely daughter but to no avail. He returned home crying and waited anxiously till the moon rose on the fifth day. He stood on the rock and gazed upwards, finding the silhouette of his pitiful daughter in the bright and clear moon. Since then, her whereabouts has been handed down and narrated by both the young and the old in the tribe. Therefore, the shadow of the moon always makes people grieved and lonely.

3. A Legend about the Maiden Who Metamorphosed into a Secretarybird

Let us tell another sad legend about the relationship between a stepmother and a daughter. One day, when her husband went out hunting, the stepmother seized the opportunity and ordered his daughter Kaboshi to fetch water. Kaboshi was obedient and went out accordingly. Being a physically weak girl, she could not find a brook from which water could be fetched even after having crossed several mountains. Gradually she felt hungry and made great efforts to return home. Before her stepmother she knelt and requested, "Dear mother, I can no longer bear the hunger. I beg you to give me a bowl of rice."

Hearing this, the stepmother stared at her in anger and replied, "People like you do not deserve even a single grain of rice. You spent too much time fetching the water, so all the leftovers have already been devoured by the dog."

Kaboshi's fragile mind could not put up with her stepmother's merciless words, and she consequently burst into tears. A moment later, when she became calmer, Kaboshi found it better to metamorphose into a bird flying in the sky at will, than to serve such a ruthless mother. She thus made up her mind. She came to the yard, held a broom beside her waist, and swung a bamboo dustpan for two to three times, and then the lovely Kaboshi incredibly transformed into a bird, lying gracefully on the twig of a tree in the yard.

Unaware of what had happened, the father came back home. Yet he could not find his daughter. He called his wife and asked, "What happened to Kaboshi? After I went out hunting, only you and my daughter stayed at home. So, you must know the whereabouts of Kaboshi."

In response to her husband's question, the stepmother pointed at the tree in the yard angrily and said, "Yes. Your lovely Kaboshi has become a bird. Look! Lying on that twig is exactly what the filially impious Kaboshi ends up."

Having never imagined that his daughter would metamorphose into a bird, the father was very depressed and cried as if he would rather die than live. Then, he took the meat of his hunted prey to that tree, weeping and saying, "Kaboshi! Kaboshi! I bring your favourite meat for you. Please transform yourself into what you were before."

However, the father's affectionate words could not be understood by the humble bird. The bird into which the daughter had metamorphosed did not even flap its wings a bit and glared at him. The father was so mournful that he simply stood there absent-mindedly. Surprisingly, as a result, his head came off his body with a loud crack.

It would be far more reasonable if it had been the head of the pitiless stepmother decollated in this way, than that of the kindly and innocent father. In spite of having become a bird, such behaviour could not be more morally despicable. Anyway, the bird into which Kaboshi metamorphosed is the ancestor of the secretarybirds we see in the world today.

4. A Legend about the Women's Forest

Once upon a time, there was a young hunter. One day he went out in the morning, walking on the grass wet with dew. Then he entered deep into a forest where there was an aboriginal tribe. The tribe had never been seen nor heard of, in which only pretty women lived. When they were playing musical instruments, the beautiful melodies lingered in the serene forest like a dream, creating a mysterious world beyond description. The young hunter was totally immersed in this incredible scene, gazing steadily at them. At this moment, a woman whispered something to other women, and then all of them surrounded the hunter gorgeously like butterflies.

"Hey! Hey! Dear young hunter, where do you come from?"

"I live outside this forest. I lost my way and came here by accident. Anyway, what is incredible is the appearance of you ladies …."

"Haha! We are the spirits of this forest called the Women's Forest, our world of freedom. Hey! Don't panic like that. What a rare visitor! Come, everybody, let us give our best to welcome this rare guest!" The women held his arms forcibly and brought him into a house where all windows were closed. After a while, the hunter went out from the house to the corridor. His face turned green, and all of his vitality utterly disappeared. In contrast, the women went out with laughter and hilarity; the magnificent music continually broke the silence in the forest.

"What? I was thinking about where you have gone. It turns out that you're here."

"Dear young hunter, we will no longer bully you. This time we will really treat you well."

"Really! Really! Come with us …."

The women said this and brought the hunter to a dining hall. However, to the hunter's astonishment, the women only inhaled the vapour without ever eating the meat and sweet potatoes in the pot. The hunter thought that perhaps those women could not appreciate the good flavours of meat and sweet potatoes. Then he took a piece of meat from the pot. As a result, the women suddenly turned hostile and looked at one another. One of them unpleasantly said, "You said that you were a hunter. This can't be true. You also said that you came from outside this forest. All of these must be a lie."

The hunter was confounded by these remarks. He then put down the chopsticks and responded, "No. I've never lied. I am really a human being."

"Don't pretend to be a human being anymore! We feed on only vapour and air. If you are a human being like us, how come you eat meat? Only boars eat meat, and only they eat sweet potatoes. Yes, you eat a boar! We are so pitiable and foolish to serve you without knowing that you are a boar …." The women's fury turned their adoration into hatred. They threw the hunter into a shed, and no woman approached there in that night. The hunter thought that all of this is his fate, so he kept silent. Nevertheless, when he listened carefully, he suddenly heard someone singing somewhere in a low voice:

How could there be lies
Between husband and wife
Loving each other?
Still alive are my eyes.
In my hands I hold a knife
Lies if there were ….

Who sang this strange lyric verse? With the help of the moonlight shining through the gaps between tree leaves, the hunter saw a charming woman standing there.

"Hey! Dear hunter from the outside, you will put your life in danger if you stay here. Please run away as soon as possible!"

"Ah! May I ask you …."

"Shush! You speak too loudly."

"You are the one who stood alone behind the trees in the distance when I was bullied by those women! Yes, you are the woman whose bright eyes are filled with a layer of the dew of fog! As such, how is it that you are here?"

"I did not belong to this forest in the past. After I got lost and entered into this forest accidentally, I became a maid of the forest's women and have since then lived in this way ...."

"Ah! So, as I have expected, you are a human being like me! A human being like me!"

"I saw you and began to miss my parents in the homeland ...."

"That's for sure! Flee this forest with me!"

"No. There is no way I can run away. I have realized that all of this is determined by fate. Oh no! It seems that the women in the house have awakened. If you still care about me, your life will be in danger. Please run away immediately!"

"Thanks! I will never forget your benevolence."

"Don't be grateful to me. All of this is caused by the forest's women's mischief. Come, run away from the gap of this fence now!"

The hunter bid her goodbye and quickly fled. He turned his head and gave a lingering look at her white face, which could still be clearly seen in the dark night.

*Originally published in *The Magazine of Taiwanese Policemen Association*, no. 90 (25 November 1924).

Taiwanese Indigenous People in the Legends (V)

1. A Legend about a Pangolin and a Monkey

There is a saying that monkeys are apparently smart. Since ancient times most people have thought that monkeys are complacent about their own wisdom. Once upon a time, a pangolin and a monkey lived in a mountain village. One day, they put fishing rods on their shoulder and went angling to a nearby river. On that day they caught a huge amount of fish which filled a large basket fully, and then went home excitedly. However, the pangolin felt unbearable thirst, so he requested the monkey to fetch some water. The monkey set out immediately as if he had already understood what the pangolin meant. A moment later he brought back a bamboo bucket of water. The pangolin took the bamboo bucket and, when he was just about to take a sip, he smelled a strong odour.

"Hey! You! Isn't this urine?"

"Don't talk nonsense! I did not fetch urine. This is really spring water. Why does it smell stinking to you? Or is it that you peed involuntarily? When the belly feels cold, we will usually pee uncontrollably …."

"Hey! To what degree are you going to make fun of me? Facts speak louder than words. Come and smell this stench!" The pangolin could not put up with the monkey's pretensions of knowing nothing about what he had done. After saying this, he took the bamboo bucket to the monkey's nose, but the monkey did not show any interest. The pangolin could not do anything with the monkey, so, without much thought, he set out to fetch water alone. Looking at the silhouette of the pangolin, the monkey revealed a guile smile on his face and said to himself, "He is so easy to deceive." Then he ate up all the fish in the basket and blunted the pangolin's arrow, making as if he had done nothing. After the pangolin returned, the monkey said to him, "Hey! When you were absent, a huge bird came and ate up all the fish. I was very angry and attempted to shoot that bird to death. But, astonishingly, the arrow was useless against the bird and was thus blunted."

After hearing the monkey's treacherous words, the pangolin—no one knew what he was thinking about—took a crutch, jumped onto the roof with alacrity, and then landed on the ground again. Proverb has it that monkeys like to imitate other people. Unwilling to admit his inferiority, the monkey immediately took the clutch as well without being aware that he had been caught in the pangolin's scheme. He jumped up and down like the pangolin, and, as a result, all the fish in his belly as well as his excrement and urine leaked out. With the undeniable evidences, even the shameless monkey confessed his crime without further verbal defence.

However, this alone could not assuage the pangolin's fury. One day, they went up the hill to burn straw. Having some ideas in mind, the pangolin pointed at the raging fire in the distance and said, "Who dares enter into the fire? You are a born coward and will probably be scared even by the sight of fire!"

Reluctant to admit defeat, the monkey was trembling with anger because of being considered a coward. "What you can do, I can do easily as well."

After hearing the monkey's words, the pangolin jumped into the straw and was surrounded by the fire set by the monkey. After a while when the fire was extinguished, he rushed out of the ashes as though nothing had happened.

"Hey! Why were you not set on fire?" asked the monkey, who found it incredible without realising that the pangolin had sneaked underground then.

"Because I was wearing dry straw."

The monkey believed what the pangolin had said and imitated him. Consequently, needless to say, when he reappeared he had already been burned to death like black charcoal. The pangolin cut his belly open, removed his flesh, and sewed the belly as it had been before. After he cast some spells, the monkey was incredibly resurrected. After awakening, the monkey found his belly strangely empty, so he began eating the meat dropped on the ground beside him with relish. Seeing this, the pangolin condemned him, "What a lunatic who eats his own flesh!" and dug through the ground. Being helpless, the monkey went to the riverside to catch fish. Nevertheless, somehow, he could not catch even a single fish on that day. He gazed vacantly at the water, and then a black-eyed monster emerged from it. The monkey fled back home desperately. The pangolin had been waiting for him with smile. "Ha …. Hey! Why are you so miserable?"

"Damn! It really sacred me. I have never seen such a kind of monster."

"Ah! The monster in the river? Perhaps the god of the water got angry because you are so lacking in virtue. Don't go to the riverside anymore. From now on let's go uphill to pluck fruit!"

"I am so happy! As I have expected, a bosom friend is the best."

On the next day, they went up the hill where there was a large tree full of mature red fruits. The monkey rapidly climbed the tree from the trunk to a twig, devouring the delicious-looking fruits alone. The pangolin, who could not wait any longer below the tree, said to the monkey, "Hey! Give me a fruit as well!"

"What? I thought you had been home but you are still here! A moment please. I will fetch you a sweet one!" The monkey threw to the pangolin a fruit which had been held in his crotch. Unaware of this, the pangolin was very pleased and took it immediately. After biting into it, it turned out to be not fragrant and sweet at all but smelled an obnoxious odour. Seeing this, the monkey on the tree laughed out loud. The so-called humaneness of Duke Xiang of Song probably applies well to this pangolin.

2. A Legend about the Origin of Tattoos

In ancient times, the mountains and the fields were full of luxuriant vegetation. In this peaceful world where fruits matured in all seasons, there was a pretty woman living alone. She sang under the shadow of trees every morning and paved a variety of grasses as her bed every night. One day, she had a child with the Earth, and after ten months gave birth to a boy like jade.

"What a tiny and lovely child …." she said near his face and fed him beautiful fruits, for she had never seen any human being other than herself. Time flowed like a current; the subsequent twenty years elapsed like a dream. Once young, she was now a thirty-five-year-old mother; the boy, once a small baby as well, also became a twenty-year-old strong man. One day, while staring at his mother working, the son said to her as if he had been reminded of something, "Dear mother! You live only with me. Don't you feel lonely? In my case, because I live only with you, I have been feeling unbearably solitary recently."

The mother glared at her son's face and, after a while, said, "You coward! Although your mother is a woman, since I was born, I had lived alone for fifteen years. Since I gave birth to you, I have never felt lonely or whatever for twenty years. Now that you are a man, how come you are so cowardly …."

"Nevertheless, my mother, recently I have been dreaming every night."

"Dreams! Dreams!"

"What? Do you, my mother, also dream? In my case, I have beautiful and happy dreams every night."

"Dreams! Dreams! The dreams are …."

When the mother was choking, the son replied with his face red, "Even before my intimate mother, I will be embarrassed if I disclose what happened in those beautiful and happy dreams. After awakening from those dreams, I felt very, very solitary."

She was unwilling to listen anymore, thinking that she understood human emotions so little. "Because I was conceived by the Nature, I have never experienced such feelings. However, my son came into existence from my own belly so that, when he grows up, he will probably want to be in love. Yes, I should begin searching for a partner for my son." Having made up her mind, from the next day on, she searched in the grasses and the woods in the mountains every day, but she could not find any woman. Disappointed, she sat on a rock as if she had been thinking about something. A moment later, she suddenly patted her knees and stood up. "As such, the only solution is for me to metamorphose into another woman and become the partner of my son."

On that day, she went back home with a cheerfulness which she had never had, and said to her son, "Today your mother found a partner who fits you perfectly well. So, go to the rock opposite that valley tomorrow morning! There will certainly be a beautiful bride waiting for you, who is lonely like you. As to your mother, I will be of no use to you after you marry a wife. So, I will go to a place several mountains away from here. Live with your wife harmoniously forever!"

The mother left home after saying these words, which the son found unbelievable. On the next day, he followed his mother's instructions and went to the opposite side of the valley where there was a beautiful and gorgeously dressed woman, with her face dyed (tattooed) black, waiting for him.

"Ah! You are my husband!"

"Ah! You are my wife!"

They held each other's hands tightly, which signified the vow between husband and wife that they would be faithful to each other forever. That is to say, as his mother, she tattooed her face in order to deceive her own son. Several hundred years have passed. Today the female descendant of Takasagozoku (Taiwanese indigenous people) must have their faces tattooed when they are about to become the wife of a man. Legend has it that this custom originates from the above story.

3. A Legend about an Uninhabited Island

After huge efforts, a man and his younger sister drifted with the current to a rock of an isolated island. Wringing out each other's clothes soaked with seawater, they calmly recalled the horrible scene they witnessed just a moment ago. The mountains collapsed deafeningly; the flames raged high in the sky; both the sunlight and the moonlight were dim, and both the people and the beasts wailed, concurring with the tumult of shaken mountains and rivers. At this miserable moment, the surging flood submerged everything. The brother and the sister were very calm and, in this violent uproar, immediately cut down a tree to make a wooden canoe. They sat in it, drifted with the waves, and picked the foxtail millet which floated towards them, handing over their lives to the fate. It was incredible that they escaped death and drifted to this small island near evening. Therefore, in relief they expressed gratitude to the god for his protection behind the scene.

"My brother, what is this island?"

The brother had been at a loss until his sister uttered a question. He looked around steadily, but there was not even a thing which resembled a house. There were no people other than they.

"Ah! There is nothing in sight. This is probably an uninhabited island."

"An uninhabited island! An uninhabited island!"

"Yes, this must be an uninhabited island. My sister, there is no need to cry like this. After all, it is thanks to the god's secret protection that we can escape from that terrible world and drift to this island. The sun has set and everywhere has been dark. Let's take a nap on this rocky seashore tonight."

The brother and the sister held each other's hand, falling asleep in coldness. After awakening, they found the glittering and dazzling sun has risen high. They thought that there might be some people living here, so they looked around everywhere but to no avail. After realising the situation, the brother encouraged the sister to build a small cabin together and farm the land by planting their remaining foxtail millet therein. Here they began a simple life. After dozens of days, on this isolated island, it was not only the sister who felt lonely. One day at night, the brother said to the sister,

"My sister, we are so unfortunate to be brought to this island by the miserable canoe of history soon after the loss of our parents. Considering the future, the solitary life on this isolated island will definitely not be happy for us. When both of us are old and our movement awkward, who will take care of us? Or if we die of illness, who will mourn our souls? My sister, don't be shocked. What I am going to say is unprecedented. Let us get married and pursue happiness and prosperity. I think this may work to repay the help the god gave us. No, I am certain that …."

Hearing the unexpected words of the brother, the sister was red-faced and stunned. They suddenly fell into silence. The bright and clear moon hid itself behind the clouds at some time, and the night at this isolated island passed in the deep sounds of the sea waves. Time passed like a current. Decades later, they already had dozens of children. Then these children married one another as well and were separated accordingly to form independent families. Finally, they established a tribe. One day, when a brother and a sister, who earned their living by casting iron, were working, the iron somehow became burning powder scattering everywhere on that day. Another couple who were farmers similarly saw foxtail millet cracking and spilling outside the mortar when bruising it. Witnessing these ill omens, these two pairs of brother and sister were afraid of getting into trouble. Therefore, they loaded their canoes with properties like iron and grain and bid farewell to their parents, brothers, and sisters,

"Dear father, mother, brothers, and sisters, cursed by the demon, we are going to a foreign country located far away at the boundary of the sky and the sea. Today is the last day we can see one another on this island where we have been accustomed to living since decades ago. Despite this, we will sail to the country hitherto unseen and then form a new tribe. We brothers and sisters will inherit our parents' warm blood lineage there, and we will be grateful for the joy of giving birth. Good bye ...."

Unfurling the sails in the south wind, a moment later the boat left their homeland island which they were to miss, disappearing in the distance on its course in the sea. Those staying on the island were the ancestors of Takasagozoku (Taiwanese indigenous people); those leaving the island were the ancestors of Taiwanese people. Therefore, that there is much less iron possessed by us Takasagozoku than that possessed by them Taiwanese people today, is not surprising. After telling this legend, the old chieftain raised the wine glass.

4. A Legend about the Worship of the Night

Once upon a time, in a mountain village there lived a very beautiful young girl named Sawa. One day, she and her older brother Arimoro were brought by their mother Bugo to the farmlands in the mountain to clear the weeds. However, the physically weak Sawa was exhausted and drowsy, falling deeply asleep under a tree at some time. She awakened after a while and found that somewhen she was placed in a large house which she had never seen nor heard of. At a loss, she looked around curiously as if it had been a dream. There a burly chieftain came leisurely before her.

"Dear young girl, from now on you are a member of our family. Do you agree? That is, you are to become my daughter!"

After hearing this, Sawa felt scared and began to weep.

"Dear young girl, no need to cry like this! Compared with being the daughter of that poor family, it is far better to be the daughter of mine, the chieftain. You are a fortunate girl."

At this moment Sawa spoke for the first time.

"May I ask you why I have been brought here?"

Asked by Sawa in this way, the chieftain's tender facial expression suddenly turned angry; his gentle voice became rude, and he roared with his face red, "You do not need to know anything about this matter. Or, if you want to know, then I may tell you. When you were sleeping under the shadow of the tree, I carried you in the arm back here. You were aware of nothing, sleeping soundly with a smile in my arms. As to your mother and brother, they fell into disorder as if they had been mad. Hahahaha ...."

Since things had happened, Sawa could do nothing but conform to the fate. Time passed like a current. The spring had left and the autumn had come for several times. Now Sawa had been an eighteen-year-old girl, shy and pretty. On a summer night, a youngster suddenly visited her family. Following the local custom, Sawa fetched some water to the guest. The young man looked at her face fixedly and said calmly, "May I ask you what your beautiful name is?"

Being in her adolescence like a flower about to blossom, embarrassment slightly spread over her face like red leaves when she was thus asked by the young man.

"I am called Sawa."

"Sawa! Sawa!"

"What? You are so surprised when hearing my name because ...."

"Because you are the sister for whom I have been searching for so many years!"

"Ah! So, you are my brother! I miss you so much! I ...."When Sawa came to the word "I," she was too happy to say anymore.

"Sawa, you no longer need to worry about anything. I have a good plan."

The brother, Arimoro, whispered something into his sister's ear. The sister, Sawa, revealed a bright smile on her face in spite of the tears in her eyes. Several days later, in the night, the tribe held a magnificent foxtail millet festival. All young men in the tribe came out to drink spirits. They let the beautiful Sawa stand at their centre, dancing as if they had been crazy. At this moment, the thorny bamboo behind them also swayed despite there being windless, on which stood a young man in resplendent clothes. With the bamboo being bent, he jumped into the centre of the crowd. He quickly held the beautiful girl in the arm and then sprang again high into the air, disappearing in the dark night. Deprived of the pretty Sawa, who had been the focus of the celebrating young tribesmen, the crowd looked at one another's face as though they had just awakened from a dream, unable to respond in time.

"Hey! Who is it that jumped down from the air a moment ago, wearing sumptuous clothes?"

"How could I know?"

"It is not within the powers of human beings to hold Sawa in the arm and spring high into the air with divine agility."

"Yes, that must be a god."

Thus, they stopped their wine festival and replaced it with a solemn altar, kneeling before it to pray. The stars twinkled in the sky like scattered diamonds, and the night in this aboriginal tribe gradually became serene ....

Postscript: If continuously unearthed, there will be many more legends like these. However, too many instalments will probably cause puzzlement to my dear readers. Therefore, here I give an end to *Taiwanese indigenous People in the Legends*. I shall think from scratch about what to write after the New Year.

*Originally published in *The Magazine of Taiwanese Policemen Association*, no. 91 (25 December 1924).

附錄一　日文原文

（61）

傳說の高砂族（一）

秋　澤　烏　川

傳說は、民族性の反映であり、不文の歷史である。私は、先年臺潯日日新報社の依囑に依り、同紙上に之が揭稿を二十數回に亘り贅表した。然し、それは公務の餘暇を以て日々書いて行つたのであるから、甚だ粗雜であつた、こと恐縮に堪へない。今囘、筆を新にして本誌に『傳說の高砂族』を執筆するに就ては、出來得る限り資料を精選し且つ記述にも注意を拂ひたいと思つてゐる。幸に些少なりとも讀者の嗜興を引、あらば、筆者の本懷である。

遠き神代の話

それは今を去る三千年の神代の昔、中央山脈ブノホンと稱す所に顏る巨大な無名の老樹があつた。その巨木の牛面は木質で他の牛面は石質、鬱蒼たる靑葉は亭々として天日を覆ひ、世は爲に常闇であつた。

——或る夏の夕暮、この樹稍化して神となり、こゝにあらゆる生物を產み玉ふた。乃ち樹幹の下部より生れ出でし一つは四脚にして身體に毛皮を纏ひ、一つは頂上に搐ありて其の形宛も樹木の如く幹に二本の枝と二本の根とを具へてゐた。次ぎに樹幹の上部より生れ出でし一つは其の形細長くして步行するなく常に匍匐し、一つは地上にあらずして空中を飛翔する翼を有してゐた。これぞ後世の人呼んで獸類・人類・蛇類・鳥類と稱するものゝ祖先である。

世は常闇の悲しさに、同じ樹から生れながらも相共に語ることが出來なかつた。ところが、或る日偶然にも一同が一つの巖窟に會合することが出來た。そこで、後世萬物の靈長

となる人間の祖先が先づ口を開いて云つた。

『皆さん、我々はこれまで風ばかり呑んで腹を滿たしてゐましたが、此の頃どうしたものか私は腹が減つて致方がなくなりました。御一統はそんな感じはせられませんか』

すると・獸類の祖先は待つてゐましたと云はんばかりに、勢ひ込んで相鎚を打つた。

『勿論・私共も最早何物か食はなければ所詮命がつゞきません。コレこの通りお腹がベコベコです』

三番目に膝を乗り出したのは、薄氣味の悪い蛇類の祖先であつた。

『然り、俺は何んでもいゝから早く呑んで腹を膨らしたい。ナア君、君も俺と同感だら

う』

聲をかけられて最後に現れたのが可愛い鳥類の祖先であつた。

『左樣です。私も皆さんのお訊の通り……』

一同の意見が一致するのを見てとつた人間の祖先は、殷に乘に告げた。

『それでは皆さんがこれから萬物を嘗め試みて、その最も自分の口に適した物を永遠の食物としやう』

その言葉が終るや否や、一同は先きを競つて地上のありとあらゆるものを嘗め試みた。

——今日我々人間や獸類や蛇類や鳥類の食物はこの時の約束事である。で、粟をその一粒を數箇に截り其の一片を鍋に入れて扱て人間の祖先は粟と肉を選んだが、粟はその一粒を數箇に截り其の一片を鍋に入れて煮る時は四五人の食料はあつた。で、粟を得るには廣い畑を排す必要もなく、僅か二三寸四方の地で人々を養ふに充分であつた。そして又肉を欲する時は、野猪を呼んで其の毛を拔き、一本を數箇に切つて同じく鍋にて煮るなれば、美味な肉が大皿に一抔盛らるゝのであつ

（63）

た。――『我れにパンを與へよ』と狂ひ叫ぶ現代に比して、それはどんなにか極樂世界であつたであらう。

閉話休題、怎うして木石二質の老樹から生れたその人類の祖先は・先づ母子相交り、兄弟相奕り、斯くて多くの子孫の繁殖を見て數年ならずして二社をなすに至つた。或る日、この甲乙二社は一河を挾みて閧の聲を揚げ、その聲に依つて人數の多少を比較した。處が、甲社の聲は乙社の聲を壓し潰さ爲に山嶽をも震動せしめた。その勢に乗じた彼等は乙社の者に向つて大呼した。

『我等のこの威勢を觀よ、我等は汝等と地を同じくするを好まず。我等は自ら山を降りて平地に出でん。汝等は剽青をなして我等と區別せよ。この差別にして汝等の氣に召さんば、よろしく我等の首を狩れよ。我等は、多數なれば敢て汝等を恐れす』

――筆者は人種的差別などといふことは、米國あたりのみの專賣特許と心得てわたが、蕃人では神代からして怎うした問題が生み出されてわたのである。彼等米人にしてこの物語を聞かば、我友を得たりと快心の微笑をその雙頬に泛べんか。乃ち平地に出でしは今日の臺灣人の祖先であつて、山に留つたのが今は高砂族とその名も莽出度く改稱せらる〜蕃人の祖先である。そうして、神代の慕は茲に静かに降される事となつてゐる。

火種を得た話

高砂族の祖先の頃は火といふのがなく、食物は皆生のまゝで食し、夜も燈火もなくて其の不自由さはとてもお話しにならなかつたつで、或る日社の重なる顔役が集つて協議會を開き、色々と智慧を絞つて見たがこれぞといふ明案も出なかつた。そこで人々は互に手分

けをして、火種を探ね求むることゝなつた。或は高山に登り、或は深谷に入り、辛苦艱難は

したけれど、夫等はみんな徒勞であつた。人々はがつかりして、山の頂上に露營の夢を結

んだ。————と、深夜に至り一人が愴惶として、大聲を揚げて呼んだ。

『火が見えた、火が見えた』

その聲に聞ならざる葦の床を飛び出した人々が遙かに沖の彼方を眺むれば、海岸を去る

沖路遙かにピカ〳〵と光る一つの火影があつた。

『〆た！』

一同は思はず愴う叫んだが、然しそれを取りに行く者

とてなかつた。そこで先づ最初に沈勇の聞が高い熊を使に立てたが、あはれ激浪の爲にそ

の牢で海底深く沈んで了つた。次には勇猛の擧れ﨑く豹を出したが、これも亦巨浪に一呑

みにせられて了つた。それを見た人々は、最早や絕望の嘆きを發した。すると、そこへ一

匹の菟仔が現れた。

『若し皆樣、私をその火種取りの使ひにやつて下さい。日頃他の獸から恥辱を受けてゐ

ます私は、命に代へてもきつと使命を果します』

男々しきその言葉に、一同は然らばとて菟仔を遣はすことゝした。彼は喜び勇んで飛鳥

の如く海に入るよと見れば、山と寄せくる波を物ともせず、沈みつ浮きつ遂に火種を取つ

て歸り來つた。一同の喜びは如何ばかりであつたか。

『おゝ勇敢な可愛の菟仔よ』

人々が感謝の辭と共に彼の脊を撫でするに、その毛竝は滑に光りを生じて今日の如く

美しくなつた。————この物語りは、日頃人々から如何に罵らるゝも隱忍自重する者は、一

（65）

悪戯神の話

朝事ある時によくほんとうの大きい力を現し得ることを教へたものであつて、それは原始時代の幼稚お伽噺とのみ見ることは出来ない。

凡そ世の中に何が厄介つて、變化自在の悪戯神ほど始末に終へないものはあるまい。然り、その神の不可思議の武器を利用して、正直一徹の人間を苦しめると云ふに至つては、全く以て沙汰の限りである。

むかし〳〵高天原にイドックといふ神様があつた。或る日のこと、徒然なるまゝに雲間から下界を覗き玉ふた處、そこには人間が住つてゐるのがアリ〳〵と見られた。

『これは面白い、俺も一つ人間の仲間入りをしてやらう』

イドックは、惡う云つてのこく〳〵天上より地上に降臨した。そして太巴聖蕃社に來り、ルメと呼ぶ美しい娘を妻に迎へた。處が彼は何を思つたのか、一目再び天に上りやがて二節の竹と、二つのババクとを持つて歸つて來た。それからといふものはイドックは畑へも出です、薄暗い家の一室に閉ち籠つて、一心に絲を繰りはじめた。その有様を見た家族の不審は元より、近隣の人々は寄ると觸るとイドックの愚かさを嘲笑した。

『いくら天から降られた神様だつて、絲ばかり繰つてゐてはお飯が食へないであらう』

『馬鹿につける藥なしとはイドックの事だ』

『だから、神様の仲間からお暇が出て、下界に流れて來たんださハッハッ……』

懲うした人々の言葉を馬耳東風と聞き流してゐたイドックは、軈て千尋の絲を繰り上げて一人山に赴き、所々に杭を打ちそれに己が繰つた絲を結びつけ、其の端を山の麓に卷き

（66）

つけ力委せに引き絞つた。――と、不可思議や百雷一時に落つるが如き轟きと共に今まで鬱蒼たりし樹木は悉く倒されて了つた。イドックは斯くてその倒れた樹木の枯れるのを待つて、山に火を放ちそれを燒き盡した。そして其の燒け跡に立つて獨樂を廻し、燒け殘り

の木樣をピン／＼と他人の畑へ投げ飛ばして了つた。

「人の畑へ木の根株を投げるとは不都合にも程がある。イドックは神にして人間の道を知らない者だ」

畑の持ち主は怒う云つて罵ぎ立てたが、何分彼の神術を恐れてゐる人々は、面と向つて如何ともするに由なかつた。そこで夜になると窃に山に上り、その根株をイドックの畑に投げ返して知らぬ顔をしてゐた。翌朝これを見たイドックはそこに立つてジャア／＼と放尿し、その根株を再び他ゝの畑へ流して了つた。そして早速その跡へ夕顔の種子を蒔きはじめた。この時、彼の義父は堪へ兼ねて云つた。

「イドックよ、父はおん身の神術には敬服してゐる。その賢いお前にして、物もあらうに夕顔の種子を蒔くとは何事であるか。米か粟かの種子を蒔いて呉れ」

「父上！暫く時期を待つて下さい。さうして收穫の喜びを待つて下さい」

斯くてその夕顔の花咲き稔る頃ともなれば、イドックは十個の殻倉を建てた。何んにも知らない養母は、女心にその狂氣じみた有樣を見るに堪へかねて姿を隠して了つた。けれどイドックはさうした事は少しも心にかけなかつた。そして自ら庭に蓆を敷いて、其の上に人間を引き連れて山に赴き、累々たる夕顔の實を採つて我家に歸り、蕃刀を以て其の實を割つた。彼は莞爾として其の人間を引き身分の體を振へば、體毛は落ちてそれが悉く人間となつた。

と、その一粒の中から粟が四五升も出で、瞬く間に庭には積んで粟の山をなし、十の倉に

《67》

は黄金色したその粟が充ち滿ちた。

『さあ、これから俺を嘲笑した奴を懲してやるんだ』

イドックは獨り言を云ひながら涯岸にやつて來た。そこには、漁に出た人々が獲物を分配してゐた。ッカ〳〵と其の前を彼が通ると見れば何んたる不思議！今まで澄潤としてゐたその魚は忽ち黒い石と化して了つた。一同は打ち驚き且つ恐れ、泣いて彼の袖に縋り前の惡口を謝した。すると、見る間にその黒い石は再び元の魚と返るのであつた。――その時の黒い石の殘りが、今日の石炭であると傳へられてゐる。

一日、祉人が耕作から歸り道、路上に美しい材木が横つてゐるので喜んで持ち歸り、屑から降さうとすれば早くもその材木はイドックとなつた。

『有難う、僕はあまり疲れてゐたので路傍に寢ころんでゐたところ、君がこゝまで肩に載せて來てくれたお陰で、きつい山路も歩かずに助かつた譯だ。ほんとに有難う』

また或る時は流れ木となつて河岸に漂ひ、人のそれを拾はんとすればヒョックリ元のイドックに返つてニコ〳〵笑ひ、又或る時は人々の耕作せる中を鹿の形をして驅け廻り、人人が鍬を投げ出してこれを追へば其の後にまはり、鍬を取つて業に隱して素知らぬ顔して我家に歸ると云ふ風に、その惡戲には何人も平の附け樣もなかつた。

――處が電光閃き雷鳴轟く日、イドックは三度び天に昇り、遂に下界には歸り來なかつた。人々は如何に喜んだことか。今日に至るまで、彼等蕃人は他人の境界を侵さず魔埃を捨てず、粟の收穫に際しては豚を屠り鷄を割きて祖先とイドックを祭り、又魚を捕りし處を他人の通行するあばら必らず之を分配する等、剽悍無比と稱せらるゝ彼等高砂族にして斯くもイドックの惡戲に挺捫つてゐるとは、またやつばり趣味深い人間生活ではないか。

（68）

女護島の話

昔、一人の漁士があつた。春の長閑な一日、竹筏に帆を張り沖へ沖へと漕ぎ出でたが、その日はどうしたものか一尾の魚も釣れなかつた。彼はがつかりして釣竿を舷に投げ、ただ茫然として海面を眺め入つたが、そこには眞黑い小島が浮いてゐるのであつた。

『お〜美しい島！あの島に上つて休まう』

彼は早速竹筏を漕ぎ寄せて、ノコ〳〵とその島に上つた。そして『これはい〜具合だ』と獨りつぶやきながら、煙草入れを腰から取り出した。と、不思議やその小島が俄に動くかと思へば、足下から大きい聲がした。

『オイ晝寢をしてゐる俺の脊の上で煙草を吸ふ奴は誰だい』

『これは驚いた。島さん、お前は人頭に口がきけるかい』

『オイ〳〵惡戯るない。俺は島ぢやあない。鯨さんだい。この馬鹿野郎！』

怎な怒號した鯨が、腹立ちまぎれに一搖體を動かしたと見れば、彼は何百里とも知れない遠い國に投げ飛ばされてゐた。そこは、彼が未だ聞きも見もしない異郷の地であつた。

然も、彼の周圍には女人ばかりが立ち竊んで、彼を物奇らしげにジロ〳〵と見てゐたのであつたが、軈て怎んな會話をはじめた。

『モシこれは何んでせう』

『何んだか人間の形はしてゐるけれど、妾達と違つて色は黑いし骨組や肉附きが大きいし、怪體の惡るい動物だわ』

『さう〳〵、これが妾達が昔噺に聞いた豚といふものかしら、一つ捕へて皆なで飼つて

（60）

見ませう』

　これを聴いて驚いたのは、彼の漁士であつた。いくら色が黒いからとと云つて、人間を豚とは情ないとホロ〳〵泣き出したが、そんなことには頓著のない女人達は、彼を小さい小屋に投げ込んで、毎日飯の殘りや芋の端のみを與へた。數日ならずして瘦せ衰へた彼は、女人達の寢息を窺つてそつと海岸に出た。そして月光隈なき遠い彼方の空を眺めて、最早や自分はあの壊しい故郷へは歸られぬかとさめ〴〵と泣き伏した。すると、そこに再び先の鯨がのつこり浮んで來た。それと見た彼は、手を合せて鯨に云つた。

『モシ〳〵鯨さん、お前さんのお蔭でとんだ憂き目に遭ひました。どうか今一度故郷に歸して下さい』

『それはお氣の毒でした。では、私の脊にお乗りなさい、早速私がお送りしませう』

　漁士は、鯨のいふまゝに彼の脊に飛び乗つた。そして鯨が二三度鰭を動かすかと思へば、床しい故郷は早や目前に見えた。

『お〳〵陸が見えた！古里の森が見えた！』

　彼が小踊りして喜ぶと鯨は云つた。

『若し人間さん！あなたが家に歸つたなら、私に何か供物を下さい』

『それは命の親だもの、私にも考へがあります』

『ちやあ、きつと約束しましたよ』

　づしんと大きい音を聞いた時は、既に彼は陸の上に投げ上げられてゐた。狂氣のやうに喜んだ彼は早速我が家に歸り、妻や我子の手を執つてあまりの嬉しさに泣き伏した。

（70）

『マァ貴郎！妻達はどんなに心配してゐましたことか。デモまあよく歸つて下さいました』

『心配をかけて濟まなかつた。俺は鯨のために、恐ろしい女護の島にやられてゐたのだ』

『女護の島！』

『誤解してはいけない。それは女人達ばかりの島ではあつたが、俺はそこで豚として假の殘りや、また著の切れ端しばかり食はされたのだ』

『妻の大事な夫を豚とは………』

『イャさう怒るナ。俺は豚にせられたばかりに怎うして歸ることが出來たんだ』

妻は『女護の島』と聽いて嫉妬の情を燃し、また『豚にせられた』と聽いて憤怒したが、最後の夫の言葉にはじめてニッコリと笑つた。

『ほんとに嬉しいこと！妻には戀しい夫、子のためには大事なお父さん！その人が今無事に歸つて來た』

妻は、無中になつて喜びに狂ひ廻つた。

『さう〳〵俺は怎うしてはゐられない。鯨に大切な約束事をして來た………』

嬥て彼は再び海岸に來つてそこに蓆を敷き、其の上に酒や餅や檳榔子などを載せて鯨を待つた。すると、遙か彼方の波間に鬱の鯨が現れだかと見れば、海水物凄くも逆立つて巨浪が一呑みにその供物を吞み去つた。——たゞ、其の時蓆のみは汀に殘り、今日に至るまで卷かれては伸び、伸びては卷かる〳〵渚の波とはなつた。そして、臺灣本島と火燒島に架せられてゐた美しい大きい橋はこの時海中に沒落し、今日の如く個々となつたと傳へ語つてゐる。

（圖）

傳說の高砂族（二）

秋　澤　烏　川

太陽征伐の話

寒帶及び溫帶地方の人々は其の寒冷を恐れる處から、赫々たる熱を有する太陽を非常に崇きものとしてこれを主神とし夜の闇を照す月を從神としてゐるが、熱帶及び亞熱帶地方になるとそれと正反對に酷暑を厭ふ處から、夜間の皎々たる月光の凉味を貪びてこれを主神とし日を從神としてゐる。而して其の酷暑の極端なる地に至つては、寧ろ太陽を敵視してゐるものさへある。本物語りの起原も、乃ちこゝに發してゐるのである。

太右、太陽が二つあつた。さうして晝夜の別なく赫々として照り輝くところ、溪は涸れ畑は荒れ、喰むべき食は絶えてあはれ人々は最早や餓死を待つより外手の盡し樣とてもなかつた。窮して神に依る人情に國の東西、昔の古今に變りなく、人々は神に祈つて救ひを求めたけれど、不幸にして其の效果は更になかつた。

「神は我々の憐みを救ふべきであるのに、かほどまで一同が赤誠を以て祈願するのに更に容るゝ處なきは、何んと云ふ無情さぞ……」

群集の中の一人が熱烈なる句調を以て斯く叫べば、一同はどつと恨の聲をあげてそれに和した。

「然り、我々は最早かゝる無慈悲なる神に依るべきでない。我々自らの事は、我々自ら

で解決すべきだ」

「醒めよ同胞！立てよ諸君！」

人々の昂憤は白熱點に達し、殺氣は天地に漲つて凄然たる雰圍氣につゝまれた。──と此時二人の青年が群集を押し分けて現れた。そして

「諸君！憂ふる勿れ。我等二人は、今より行きて太陽を射殺するであらう。冀くば暫時の苦痛を忍び、今日の悲憤の歡喜となるの日を待ち給へ」

と云ひ終るや、彼の二青年は粟と朱藥を携へて、男々しくも太陽征伐の旅路に上つた。

──廣袤迢る幾萬里、星霜重ぬ幾十年、彼等は辛苦艱難漸くにして地の端に達する事が出來た。喜び勇んだ二青年は嚴上に立ちて弓を番へ、今や遲しと太陽の昇るのを待ち受けた。

やがて、赫々たる鐵を熔した如き眞紅の太陽は海の彼方に現れ出でた。勇敢なる二青年はこゝぞと颯と切つて放てば、二本の征矢は誤たず太陽の中央を美ん事射貫いた。悲痛凄慘──見る〳〵淋漓たる血汐は瀧津瀨の如く降り下り、大和田輝美には紅の潮が泡立つた。

さるにても哀れをとめし、その太陽の血汐に打たれて海中に落ちた一青年の死であつた。

殘る青年は太陽を射し喜びも友を失ひし悲しみに、憤然として一人淋しく歸路に就いた。そして二人が征途の道々に捨て來つた朱藥の實の生へて大木となり、累々として榴に實を結べるも今は亡き友の悲しい思出として、その道しるべを辿り漸く我が家に歸りを受けた。

──と、遂に我れの征途を辿り呉れし父母は既に此の世の人にあらず、門に迎へる老人の我が友であるのに驚きながら、父母のありし日の物語りにせめての心の手向けとした。

「さあ我等の生命の恩人を迎へよ」

「我等は〻この恩人に依つて夜を得たのである。涼を得たのである。夜あつてこそ人生

（71）

は樂しく、凉あつてこそ作物は稔るのである」

『然り！而して其の赫々たる功績を千右に傳へよ』

岐々たる月光のもとに人々が喜びと感謝に酌む盃の重なりゆけば、一人の老翁は檀上に立つて天を仰いで云つた。

『諸君！諸君は今我等の頭上に輝く月と星を知るや。太陽二つありて夜のなかりし今は昔となつた日は、天に照るは我等を苦しめる太陽あるのみであつたのだ。然るに、勇敢なるこの青年が太陽の一つを射落した時、四方に散つた血潮が天に止まつて月と星とになつたのである。今夜に怨うして月光の凉を睞ひまた星塵の美を賞し得るのも、乃ちこの青年の賜である。』

拍手は雷のやうに起つた。凉風の絶えず綠蔭に薰る處、熱狂せる人々は夜の更くるのも知らず盃の數を重ねた。

日ご月ご星の話

樹靈宿るといふ大きい老檜を伐り倒した父はほつと息を吐いたが、軈て運搬に餘念のない息子の兄弟に云つた。

『どうも喉が渴いて致方がない、溪に行つて水を汲んで來て吳れ』

父の命に兄弟は竹筒を以て谷間に降りて行つたが、常に湛湛として澄める溪流は其の日に限り降雨もないのに眞黑に濁つてゐた。兄弟はその水の流れを見て不思議に思つたが、深くも探らず其の儘歸り來つて父にその山を告げた。父は只苦笑するのみで何んと答へなかつたが、やがて其の日も暮れ翌日再び父の命に溪に行つたところ、やつぱり前日と同じ

く流れは濁つてゐた。斯くて翌々日三度行くも、水は益々濁る一方であつた。――この兄弟の訴を聽いた父は奇怪の眉をひそめたが、暫くして靜に口を開いた。

「それは必らず上流に惡戲をする者がゐるに相違ない。牛か豚かそれとも人間か、二人は行つて容赦なくそれを斬り捨てよ」

そこで兄弟は快心の色をなして溪間に降り上流を探ぬるに、果してそこには父の言葉の如く一人の男が頭を股間に挿みて水を濁してゐた。これを見た兄弟は憤怒に馳られて不意打ちに彼の男を倒し蔵首したが、扨てよくく見ればこは何事ぞ！その首は自ら斬り捨てよと命じた現在の父であつた。斯くと知つた兄弟は狂せんばかりに打ち驚き且つ嘆き悲しんだが、今となつては所詮せんすべともなかつた。泣くく我が家に歸り母にこの由を語れば「汝等は父の首を狩り得るほどの勇あらば、他人の首を得るは容易であらう。さあ今より直に蔵首に赴け。さうして數百の首を得るにあらざれば家に歸るを許さず‥‥」と

て、怒氣荒々しく兄弟を戶外に突き出した。二人はさめくとそこに泣き伏したが、軈て弟は兄の肩を撫でく云つた。

「兄さん、かうなれば私共は母上の御言葉に從つて多くの首を狩り、せめては亡き父上の靈を慰め又母上の勘氣を解かねばなりません。それには卑南社の人々は勇猛にして、數を見れば何處までも追及すると聞きますれば、私共は彼等のその特性を利用して加納納の谷に誘ひ出し、石柵を設けて一潰しに數十人の首を得やうではありませんか」

「お～弟よ！お前は大變よい處へ氣がついた。それでは早速その戰陣に出立しやう」

そこで兄弟二人は深山幽谷に豹を狩つて其の血を携へて卑南社に到り、蕃童の熟睡を見澄して不意に發砲して其の三名を倒した。時ならぬ銃聲に夢を破つた蕃社の人々は、早く

（ 73 ）

も兄弟を見出して銃槍を手に追跡して來た。　兄弟は我が事成れりと携へ來つた豹の血を逃

ぐる道々に落し、この身の負傷せるもの〳〵如く裝ひつゝ人々を誘ひ出し、溪の兩岸に橋の

如く籐を張り其の上に大石を置けるを一時に切つて落とし、褥然たる響と共に追ひ來る數

十人を一時に殺して了つた。　斯くてその首を携へて我が家に歸り、父の亡靈に供へて母に

罪を謝し一人の妹と共に其の前で舞踏をはじめた。

――と、不思議や兄弟妹の三人の足は先づ地中に入り、次に腰を沒しやがて腰にまで及

んだ。かくて次第に身の地中に落ち行き、今や肯をも沒せんとするや三人は聲を揃へて母

に云つた。

　『私共は思ふまゝ父上の亡靈を祭り母上の御心を慰め得ましたので、最早や何事も申し

遺すことゝてもありません。さらば、私共は斯く歌ひ舞ひながら地中に入ります。今夕山

に登る月は兄、明朝東天に出づる日は弟（こゝにても『太陽征伐の話』に記せるが如く月を

主とし日を從としてゐるのを見遁してはならない）そして中空の闇にキラ〳〵と輝く大き

い星は妹でムいます。さらば母上、永遠に御機嫌よろしく……』

　嬢て、三人は歌ひながら地中に姿に沒して了つた。冬の日の暮れ足早く暮靄紫にたちこ

むれば、東山の端に皓々たる月が出で、須臾にして其の光りも優しき星は輝き染め、鶏聲

ほがらかに曉を報ずれば、赫々たる太陽は東天に昇つた。……斯して一箇月に一回兄の

月と弟の日は相接近してお互にその安否を問ひつゝ、限りなき道程を何時迄も〳〵辿ると

語り傳へられてゐる。

雷電になつた話

むかし或る山里に、仲よく暮してゐる三人の親子があつた。ところが一日、その父と子が朝早くから獵に出でたまゝ、夕暮れになつても歸つて來なかつた。母はほの暗い燈火の下で、若しや恐ろしい獸に食はれはしなかつたか、若しや深い溪に陷りはしなかつたかと、安心に夫や、我が子の上を案じ煩つてゐた。――と、夜も更けて行つた頃、我が子が一人情然として歸つて來た。

「あゝよく歸つて吳れました。お母さんは、どんなに心配してゐましたことか。さあ、早くお上りなさい。そして、お父さんは……」

父はと問はれて、その子はしく〳〵と泣き出した。

「二人は道を踏み迷ひ、私は遂にお父さんを探すことが出來ず、惌うして一人で漸く歸つて來ました」

「何！お父さんを一人山の中に遺してお前一人歸つて來た？お前はまあ何んといふ親不孝者ぞ。姿は見えずとも、父の名を叫べば答へがあらうに……」

「イェいくら呼んでも、お父さんの應へはありませんでした」

母はこの言葉を聽くと怒氣荒々しく、自ら松明に火を點じて更け行く夜の霧を衝いて夫を探ねに出た。そして、とある谷間に漸く夫を見出した彼女は狂喜して夫に抱きついた。

「あゝよく生きてゐて下さいました、それにしても不孝者はあの子！」

我が家に歸り來つた父は、妻よりの訴を聽いてその聲荒々しく

「お前は何んといふ不孝者ぞ。叫ぶも應へがなかつたと云ふが、この父の聲はお前の耳には入らぬか。全山に響くこの聲！お前が惌うした大聲で呼ぶのに、この父が何んで答へ得ない事があらうぞ。聽け、この聲！この聲！」

（75）

無中になつて憑う怒號したが、軈て母の手を執つてそのまゝ天に昇つて了つた。そして父は雷となり、母は電となつた。乃ちその時の父の聲は雷鳴であり、母の聰明は電光であるこ今の世まで語り傳へられた。

天を高めた王鳥の話

高砂族の祖先の頃は、天がほんの手近かにあつたので、人々は地上にゐることが出來す地中に穴を掘つて生活してゐた。從つて其の不便苦痛は限りなく、どうかして廣い地上に愉快に暮したいものだと、或日協議會を開いた。然し、我れこそ其の使命を果さんと名乗り出づる者とてもなく、一座は深い吐息にのみ囚はれて行つた。――と、席末から一人の少年が進み出て口を開いた。

『太陽の苦熱を去らしめんとするには、先づ天を上方に揚げる外とるべき道がない。それには、地に棲んでゐる我々人間や獸類では何の役にもたゝない。この大任を果すものこそ、天を翔る鳥類を措いて外にない。希くば、先づ鳥といふ鳥を殘らず呼び集めて、その上で更によき方策を講じていたゝきたい』

一同は、この少年の奇智に思はや柏手喝采をしたが、軈て長老は天に向つて大聲を發して云つた。

『世の總ての鳥達よ！汝等寸時も早く來つて我等の謀議に與かれ！』

その聲を聞きつけた鳥達は、何事であらうと先を競つて人々の前に集つた。そこで長老は嚴に彼等に告げた。

『鳥達よ！お前等も見るが如く、今日の天地は其の間が極めて近く、日々太陽の爲めに

焦死する者が數知れない。それがため・我々も斯く地中に穴を掘つて棲んでゐる次第であ
る。お前達としても、かうした不便と苦痛を欲するのであるまい。さうだ、天が高ければ
お前達は思ふ存分雲際遙に飛翔し得るであらう。我々としても、自由に地上に出づるを得
るのであらう。我々とお前達のために、天を高く昇らしてこの灼赫たる炎熱の苦より避け
しめよ』

茲に於て、先づ第一に進み出でたのが鳶であつた。

『それは、お易い御用だ。僕が空中で二三度羽搏をすれば、天はその煽りに高く飛び去
るのだ』

高慢な鳶は、懸う大言壯語して空高く舞ひ上り勢よくバタ〳〵と羽搏をしたが、天は一
向そんなことに驚く樣子もなかつた。鳶は顏を掻き〳〵降りて來た。次に現れたのは鴉で
あつた。

『ハッハッ……皆さん！目ほどにもない鳶君の態を御覽なさい。私はもと太陽の中に
棲んでゐたので身體こそこんなに黑く焦げちやつたが、それだけ太陽と私は仲好しなんだ。
で私が直々一つ相談して來やう』

鴉は戀して太陽めがけて飛んで行つたが、しかし何時迄經つても歸つて來なかつた。

『鴉もやつぱり駄目かナ』

人々は顏を曇らした。最の少年も此度は不安の色を滿へて數々の鳥を見渡した。――と
そこへ小さいタタチユといふ鳥がちよこ〳〵と進み出た。これを見た他の鳥達は、互に袖
否羽を引き合つて嘲笑した。

『見玉へ、馬鹿な奴は致方がないよ。アノ小ぼけなタタチユがよくも鐵面皮に出られた

（77）

ものだ』。

　『ほんとに我身を知らざるタタチュ、恥も外聞もないのだから寧ろ可憐さうよ。アノ勇猛な鵄君でさへ失敗し、また太陽と火の伸好しの鴉君さへ滿足に歸つて來ないのに……』

　さうした鳥達の嘲笑を耳にもかけないタタチュは、やがて小さい可愛い軀に全身の力を込めて『タッチユカ、タッチユカ、タッチユカ……』と囀き出した。その聲の凉しさ、清らかさ、朗らかさ。人々は無中になつて聞き惚れてゐた。するとその聲は次第に四方に懷きひろがり、天地は爲に震動して夫はみる〳〵高く上層に昇つて行つた。

　――今日我々がやすらかに地上に棲息し得るのは、實にこの小鳥の賜である。さればこそ其のタタチュは萬鳥の王となり、幾千年の星霜を經たる今が世まで、神の鳥として崇め敬されてゐるのである。

風と雨と雪の話

　ある日、風と雨と雪が集つて力自慢をはじめた。

　『凡そ世の中に、俺ほど力の強いものはあるまい。俺の向ふところ、森羅萬象悉く風靡せざるはなしだ』

　先づ怒う云つて、高慢さうに高くもない鼻をピョつかせたのは風であつた。そして、それを受けて膝を乘り出したのが雨であつた。

　『俺は風君のやうに荒つぽくはないが、その泛々として土に入る力は大山もよく崩し得るのだ。そこへ行くと、雪君は女のやうに白い顏をしてゐるばかりで、皆目駄目なんだね』

　『然り、雪君は我友とするには、あまりに貧弱だハッハッ……』

雨と嵐の嘲笑を默つて聽いてゐた雪は、この時はじめに口を開いた。

「或程僕の身體は、女のやうに白い。そして、嵐君のやうに處へ處がないでもなく、ま
た雨君のやうにジメ〳〵と陰氣でもない。僕が赴く處は總て銀世界となつて、その寒烈は
骨を利さなければやまない。僕から見れば、君達の力はほんの戲れ事に過ぎないのだ」

これを聽いた雨と嵐は柄にもなく眞赤になつて怒つた。

「よし！それでは實際に三人の力を比較して見やう」

氣早やな嵐は、憑う云つたかと思ふと、己の下腹に力を込めて颯と吹き出した。と、天
地は鴛めに鳴動して石は飛び木は倒れ、雲は早瀬の樣に流れて物凄い光景を呈した。

「オイ、どんなもんだい。俺の力は偉大だらうハッハッ……。雨君、君も一つ大きく
やつて雪奴を驚かしてやり玉へ」

おいと答へて雨がやがて浦然として降り出したので、見る〳〵うちに谷は溢れて濁流は
瀧の如く下つた。

「ヒャ〳〵、雨君の腕前天晴々々」

嵐は手を拍ちながら、伺ほも憑うした憎まれ口を叩いた。雪はニコ〳〵笑ひながら見て
ゐたが、甦て自分の番になると如何にも物靜かに、森々として白羽を散らすが如くに降り
出した。――と、今まで靑々としてゐた草も木も俄に枯れ、見渡す限り山も野も白皚々水
は氷り樹葉は凍へ行くに、嵐や雨の高慢ぶりを嚴窟の中で嘲笑してゐた人々は恐
れ戰き、遂に雪の前に平伏した。この有樣を見た嵐と雨ははじめの勢ひは何處へやら、い
つしかこそ〳〵と逃げ去つて了つた。

――山間の高地に住んで嵐や雨の恐ろしさを知らない彼等高砂族が、如何に寒さを怖れ
てゐるかは、この小さい物語にも窺ひ知ることが出來やう。

（66）

傳説の高砂族（三）

首狩の始つた話

秋澤　島川

開けゆく大御代の光り洽く、南溟の孤島の深山奧ふかく棲む酷暑さへ惠みの露に潤ふ有難さよ。時は今日を去る三千年の昔、ニブヌと申す神が新高山に降臨ましまして茲にはじめて人間を造り玉ふた。處がその當時の人間は神の御手製だけあつて極めて純潔、從つて不老不死ともいふべき程の長壽を許されてゐた。だから若し過つて死ぬるやうなことがあつても、ニブヌの神の御力に依つて蘇生することが出來たっ且つ、さうして神の御術を頼すことが五囘に及べば、最早やこの世に用なきものとして御暇が與ることとなつてゐた。それは、過ちとは云へ五囘も續けて死ぬる者は、徐程命の欲しくない者と神樣が見切りをつけられるからであらう。

閑話休題、一日ニブヌ神が何か急用があつて二囘目に死亡した者をその傍家に殘して外出して了つた。處が其の後にヒェンハと云ふ極めておせつかいな神樣が來て亡者に取りすがり悲しみ止まず、遂に家中に穴を掘つて屍を埋め、其の上に土を蔽ひて泣き伏した。所用を果して歸り來つたニブヌの神はこの有樣を見て大いに驚いたが、最早やヒェンハの神が泣いた後だから如何ともするに由なかつた。星霜移る三千歳・彼等が死者を家中に埋めその上に泣き悲しむならはしに今も尙ほ變りがない。

（67）

——その事あつて以來、人間は何時でもコロリ死を賜ふ光榮を有するに至つた。だが

それでも人間の繁殖力は素晴らしい勢で、その粗製濫造の結果は性質のよくない奴が飛び

出す樣になつた。そこでニブヲの神は、彼等惡人を除く手段として大洪水をおこし、漫々

たる濁水を四方に漲らした。さうして丘陵も見る／＼濁水に呑まれ行くに、人々は漸く遁

れて再び新高山の頂に集つた。

『隨分ヒドイ水だナ』

『見渡す限り濁流奔眞に愉快ちやあないか』

『オイ／＼滅らず口は止せやい、神樣のお氣に障るんだぞ』

その時分から瓢漢な吞氣者もあれば、神萬能の神經家もあつた。

『腹が滅つたナァ』

一人が思ひ出したやうに憩う云ふと、他の人々は急に腹を抱へて『空いたナァ』と相槌

を打つた。殼類なく野獸を獵して常食としてゐた當時のこととて、この大水では所詮食を

求むることが出來なかつた。——と、一人の壯者が自分の飼つてゐた犬を屠つた。この有

樣を見た先きの瓢漢者は、その犬の首を竹竿に刺して人々の間を振り歩いた。中には眉の

根を顰める者もあつたが、其の多くの者は面白い／＼と手を拍つて喜んだ。

『アノ竹の先きの犬の首を見い』

『首ばかりでも一人前に目を睜つてゐらァ』

『體のない方が奇らしくて面白いや』

こんな人々の言葉を聞いた瓢漢先生は、愈々調子に乘つて今度は猿を殺してその首と犬

の首と変換した。人々は盆々面白がつて、その奇抜を賞し合つた。

（68）

「猿の首でもこんなに面白い、若しこれが我々と同じ人間の首だつたら、どんなにか愉快な事であらう」

「フン、今まで大きい顔をして意張つてゐた奴が・コロリと参つて青い顔を竹竿の先きに晒す處は、どんなに痛快か知れない」

「面白いや、面白いや」

既に殺氣に滿ちた一同は、その頃社人間の憎まれ者だつた惡黨を殺し其の首を同じ竹の先きに刺して我を忘れて踊り狂つた。――その馘首踊りが神の御意に叶つたのか、水は俄に減じて丘陵も見へ野も現れた。

「さあ水が引いた、良い地へ行かうっ そして我々は一隊となつて他の社の首を狩り集めやう。我々の社の者の首でさへこんなに面白いのだから、敵の首を取るはどんなに愉快であるか知れない」

人々は手に手に武器を携へて、曉の霧を衝いて新高山を下つた………。

分家の始つた話

むかし竈に親孝行のトマイコールといふ若い獵人があつた。風の晨も雨の夕べも山に狩りする傍ら畑を耕し、その獲たる處のものを父に棒ぐるのを何よりの喜びとしてゐた。――ある日のこと、彼は常の如く銃を肩に星光を踏んで家を出たが、その朝は霧が雲のやうに深く山路をつゝんでゐた。端ぎ登る彼はその霧を吸つて、思はずハックションと嚔をした。と、同じく霧の中でハックションと嚔をする者があつた。

「オヤ、この山には僕より外に人はゐない筈だのに、いまの嚔は訝しいナ」

（69）

トマイコールは獨りつぶやきながら、四方を探したがやつばり人影は見へなかつた。

『訝しいナ』

その時、霧の中でまた慇ふ云ふ聲がした。彼はその聲を目標に再び探ねた處、そこには百日紅が今を盛りと咲き亂れてゐた。トマイコールはその前に立つてじつと花を眺めてゐたが、やがて言葉をかけた。

『今僕の口眞似をしたのは、お前だつたかい』

するとその百日紅は同じく『今僕の口眞似をしたのは、お前だつたかい』と言葉を返した。それを聞いた彼は

『樹の分際で人の口眞似をするとは何事だ！』

と云ひも終らず、腰の一刀をスラリと拔いた。と、ホロ〳〵と散る百日紅の花の中から

『しばらく……』と聲がか〻つた。

『若き殿よ！木を伐るとも、妾を傷づくること勿れ』

こ〻にはじめて木の中に人のゐることに氣づける彼は、百日紅を根本から伐り倒した。すると果してその斬り口から、美しい一人の女が現れた。

『オヤ貴女はどうしてこ〻にゐられしや』

トマイコールがいぶかしさに驚けば、美女は莞爾として云つた。

『妾、この百日紅の精なのよ。妾は一度世の中に出て見たいと思つてゐたけれど、どうしてもこの木から脱け出すことが出來なかつたの。それが今日殿のお薩で妾の日頃の思ひが達せられて〻こんなに嬉しい事はない。この御恩返しに妾は殿の……イヤ妾を妾とす

ることをお赦し下さい』

（70）

百日紅の散り敷く木の下に夫婦の契りを結んだ二人は、そこにさゝやかなる草の庵を結んだ。然し、孝行者のトマイコールは、夫婦の愛のために父を忘れゝことはなかつた。晨に夕べにその庵から溪を渉つて父の家に歸り、耕作をしては夜に入ると戀しい妻の待つ庵へと歸り行くのであつた。その有様を見た父はあまりのいぢらしさに、或る日彼を膝元に呼んで云つた。

「トマイコールよ、お前の至らざるなき孝養はよくよくこの父が承知してゐる。で、もう今日までのやうに毎日父の家に來なくてもいゝ。昨今のやうに大雨が降つては、溪水も汎濫しやう。第一、危險この上がない。それで、お前が若し山で鹿を狩り得たならば、其の頭を持つて來て吳れ。さうしてお前達二人が何時までも伸よく暮してくれることが、この父への何よりの孝養である」

トマイコールは、其の後鹿を捕へたならば必らず父の家を訪ひ、その一日を父の家に暮すのであつたが、歲華は流水と去り逝きて、トマイコールは今は年老ひ溪を渉ることさへ自由ならざるやうになつた。そこで父は彼に一の神像を興へ、獵に出でし時は獸の頭骨を以て神を祭れと命じ、竝に父子は全く別々に一家をなして餘生を靜かに途つた。──これが、彼等高砂族の分家の始つた由來であると語り傳へられてゐる。

獨木舟の話

今や臺灣電力株式會社の工事に伴ふ問題の中心となつてゐる彼の太古ながらの碧水を湛ふる日月潭に浮ぶ獨木舟につき、こんな物語が傳へられてゐる──。

むかしく──極めて伸のいゝ五人の若者があつた。一日五人が打ち連れ立つて中央山脈の

（71）

奥深く狩獵に出かけたが、どうしたものか其の日は一匹の獲物もなかつた。然し日はさうしたことに頓著なく最早や西に傾いて、蕃山の壁々は紫に耀つてゐた。力ぬけのした五人はある大きい巌の上に腰を掛けて、ボンヤリ暮れゆく光景を眺めてゐた。そして、深山の沈獸に溶け合つたかの様に、五人は口をつぐんでゐた。――と、何處から來たのか一匹の白鹿が電光のやうに目の前を駈け去つた。身動きもしなかつた五人の若者は、それと見ると、忽ち立ち上つて其の後を追つたが、白鹿は途に日月潭に出た。そうして飛鳥の如く水の中に躍り込み、やがて沈みつ浮きつ潭の浮き島に泳ぎ渡つた。若者は汀に突つ立つたま〃、夢でも見てゐるかのやうにじつと水面を眺めてゐたが、不思議やそこに樟楠木の破片に乗つた鼠が現れた。これを見た五人の若者は、はじめて口を開いた。

『モシ〳〵水の上の鼠さん・あなたは如何してそんな小さい木の切れに乗つて沈まないのかね』そして前へ行くときはどうして進むのかね』

鼠は若者の聲にジロリ後を振り向いたが、黙つたま〃自分の尾を舵として沖へ沖へと出て行つた。

『全く不思議だね』

『一體如何してこの深い水の上に浮ばれやう？』

『底は何百尺とも知れぬ潭だ。どうしてそれが渡れやう？』

『イヤあれは神樣なんだ。夢々疑つてはならぬ』

『さうだ、我々はその神の御敎を眞似てこの水を渡らう』

そこで五人は、大きい樹を刳りて舟を造り、板を削りて舵を作り、夕燒け映ゆる潭に浮かせば、舟はよする小波に静にゆれた。五人の若者は喜び勇んで舟に飛び乗つたが、その

（72）

ふはりとした浮き心地は所詮山嶽を棄足で上り下りする彼等の未だ味はない愉快さであつた。若者達は子供のやうに嬉々として、舷の水を手にかきながら、見る〳〵沖の浮き島に渡り着いた。そして、さきに逃げ失せた白鹿を捕へて首尾よく元の岸に歸つて來た。この有樣を木の間から覗つてゐた土人は、若者が舟から上ると走り出て云つた。

『君、それは大變便利なものだね。僕に一つ讓つて吳れないかね』

『オイ出しぬけに何んだい。大きい聲をして』

『イヤこれは失敬。實はね、君達はこんなものを持つては所詮あの高い山を越へて歸れまいと思つたから、僕がこゝにいゝ〳〵肉を持つて來た。さあこれと君の舟と交換しやう』

『オイ〳〵人を馬鹿にするない。そんな客唾い肉と、この舟と交換してたまるかい。我々は、そんな間拔け野郎ぢやあない。アゝ、あの乗り心地！僕等は、それに乗つて歸るのだ』

若者は、怎う云ひながら舟を陸に引き揚げた。そして早速それに飛び乗つたが、此度は舟がふはりともせず、何の乗り心地のいゝこともなかつた。そして、手を打ち振り〳〵したけれど、舟は一寸も進まなかつた。五人の若者達は、互に顔を見合して泣き相になつた。

それと見た土人は

『ソン、ちやあ僕は歸らう。君等はそれであの高い酢を越へて歸り玉へ』

と意地惡く云つた。若者五人は頭をかき〳〵舟と肉と交換した。そして暮れゆく木の間に消へて行つた。——今宵ほあの紺青の水に浮いてゐるその詩的な獨木舟も、愈々水力電力の工事が完成の曉は、やがて跡形もなくその姿は失はれるであらう。

（註）

豫言者の話

カサウタモは、次第に衰へ行きて最早や餘命幾程もなきと悟るや、病褥より遑ひ出でて父母の前に兩の手をついて云つた。

「お父さんお母さん、永々エラィ御世話になりましたが、私は到底囘春してお二人にお仕へすることが出來ません。人の子として、これほどの不孝がまたとありませうか。然し、私は決してこのまゝ御兩親を見捨て申すのではありません。若しこの僕私の呼吸は絶え、身體は冷めたくなりましても、右の拇指が自ら動けば、必らず再び生れ返つてお二人に孝養を盡します。萬一、指の動かないやうな事がありましたなら、その時こそは永遠に死んだものだと思つて下さい……」

彼は斯く言ひ終るや、靜かに眼を閉ぢ眠るが如くに息を引き取つた。然し、その拇指は不思議にも微に動いてゐた。父母は深き悲しみのうちにも、せめて我子の再生の日を思ひその骸に取りすがつて介抱に心をつくした。――一日より三日の朝までは漸次その指の動きは鈍り行くのみであつたが、三日の午後に至り少しく動き方ゞ早め、五日目の夕暮れ時より徴に呼吸をはじむと見るうちに、カサウタモは徴笑をふくんで再生した。父母兄弟の喜びと驚きは如何ばかりなりしぞ。人々は彼を取り圍んで再生を祝した。

「お父さんお母さんさうして兄弟の皆さん、私はこの五日以前息を引き取る時、天から神樣が降りて來られ私の名を呼び手を執りて そのまゝ私を天に伴ひ昇られました。初めて見た天上の美しさ、珍らしさ、とてもお話はできません。御堂眩き中におはす神々の容さよ。金繡の衣かゞやく舞ふ天女の美しさよ。ほんとに、下界の人々の想像だにも及ばん佳麗

（74）

の歓樂境！」

『コレ〳〵お前はこの神様と一處に今まで暮してゐたかえ』

『お母さん喜んで下さい。私は五日間といふものは全く夢中で暮しました。』

『さりやあお前は欲しかつたか知れないが、俺達はお前が忠を引き取つてから、如何な

に心配したか知れないのだ』

『お父さん、安神して下さい。その代りに、私は下界人の未だ夢にも知らない奇術を教

へられて來ました』

『奇術！奇術！』

『兄弟の皆さん、まあ默つて聽いて下さい。今も申しました綺麗結構な宮殿の中に殊に

目立つて威容正しき神様が私を招かれて、お前は人間界の豫言者となれ、それに要する奇

術を只今授け得させであらう……と仰せあつて、お手づからその奇々怪々の術を傳授し

て下さいました。で私は、惜しき天國を後にしてこの下界に歸り來つたのであります』

人々は、扨ても不思議のことよと、その奇術を選んで止まなかつたが、カサウタモは「神

のお告げである。扨もなきに施すことは出來ない」と、容易にその術を行ふとはしなかつ

た――。然し、其の後に至つて人間界に起る諸現象を豫知して人の禍を救ひ、出獄の時の

獲物の有無多少を卜し、年の豊凶、行方不明者の所在を占し、一つとして適中せないもの

とてなかつた。

蓋しこのカサウタモこそ、豫言判斷者の祖であつて、彼等高砂族に於ては、豫言卜占は

乃ち神の奇術であると信じてゐる。

（46）

傳説の高砂族（四）

鶴になつた二神の話

秋　澤　烏　川

　むかし〱〜高天原にマダビラ、リスンと云ふ男女兩柱の神があつた。一日南方のある高嶺に降臨し玉ひ、そこに四男二女を擧げた。處が母神がその二女を懷妊した際、腹部より爆然たる光りを放ち、體内ためにやうに水晶のやうに透き徹つてゐた。やがて月滿ち産れ落ちたのはその奇蹟に違はず花よりも美しい女神であつた。父母の二神は殊の外二女の彼女を愛くしみ育て〱〜ぬたが、歳華は流水の如く小やみもなく流れ逝き、彼女は早くも十八歳の春を迎へたのであつた。――ある日のこと、彼女は常の如く一人水汲みに谷に降りて行つた處が不思議やそこにはこれ迄で見たことのない一人の美少年が立つてゐた。そして、逃げ去らんとする彼女の袖を捕へて云つた。

　『私は、決して怪しい者ではありません。質は海の神様の命を受けて、姬をお迎へに参つたのでムいます。……と申し上げたばかりではお判りになりますまいが、質は海の神樣がせひ姬を后宮に致されんとの深い思召でムいます。今日より五日の後、私が再び茲に姬をお伴ひ申しに参りますっ。どうか、御用意をしてお待ち下さいませ』

　慈う云ひ終るや否や、美少年の姿は搔き消す如くなくなつて了つた。未だ春を解せぬ彼女は、そのありし次第を父母に落ちなく物語つた。と、父母の歎きはいかばかりぞ、早速木

（47）

箱を造り彼女をその中に入れて固く蓋を閉ぢた。しかし、彼女の體內より發する光りは燦然としてその木箱を徹し、外まで漏れるのであつた。二重三重と木箱はかさねられたが、やつばり彼女の美しい姿は外からアリ／＼と認められた。されば今度は地中に穴を掘り、これに彼女を埋めて見たが、燦然たる光りはやつばりその地を水晶の如く照した。父母の二神は、その上に坐して夜も眠らずこれを守つてゐたが、五日の夕方までは何等の異變とてもなかつた。父母兄弟はそれに安神して、兄の二人が庭に出でて粟を搗きはじめた。

……と、日に觀る＼竹の音の暮れ行く空に響けば、忽ち一天かき曇り、木々は醒風に身を震はしておの／＼き伏し、見る／＼うちに山の如き巨浪が押し寄せて來た。家も人もその濁流に吞まれ去るを、幸にもその親子は山上に遯る＼ことが出來た。然し、大事な二女の姿は遂にその子の中に見出されなかつた。父母の二神は狂氣の如くに、娘の名を叫びつ＼山上より遙かに彼方の海を眺むるにこはそも如何？そこには、彼女が海神に伴はる＼姿がアリ／＼と見えた。父母兄弟は、聲を限りに泣き叫んだ―――と、彼女にその聲が達したのか遙かに山上を顧みて云つた。

『お父さま、お母さま、さうして兄弟の皆さま、今になつて、いかほど泣き悲しんだとて、姿は海神の手から遯る＼ことが出來ません。お父さまやお母さまやそして兄弟の皆樣と一所に樂しく暮す日は永遠にありません。けれど、何事も運命でムいます。もうお泣き下さいますな。』

彼女は斯く言ひ終るや、我れと我が腕を切り取つて海中に投げた。と、その腕は一尾の魚となつて波の中に深く泳ぎ去つた。

『ねえお父さま、お母さま、兄弟の皆さま、姿し海神のもとに參りますれば、毎日お米を搗かねばなりません。姿し搗く杵の音！それは、天に昇つて雷となるでせう。今後、天に電光閃き雷鳴を聞けば、姿が一人淋しく米を搗いてゐると思つて下さい──』

彼女の美しい姿は、そのまゝ海中深く沒して了つた。親子は泣き狂ひながら水の引くのを待つたが、濁流は益々増すばかりであつた。そこで一同に兄弟は疲れ、とある地に留つたが、父母の二神は伺ほも北の嶺を越えて、漸くのことである低地に達した。其處より末だ見ぬ粟稔る地を尋ねて行つた。途中にて水地に足を入れながら、彼女の姿の沒した紺青の水を湛へた海を眺めてゐたが、不思議や身體に羽が生え、その姿はいつしか美しい鶴となつて・やがて空高く飛び去つた。二神は、その──その故に今日もなほは孤鶴は見ず、必らずや一對うち連れて飛び舞ふ芽出度さにあり

と語り傳へられた。

月に入りし娘の話

今は昔、加禮宛社に一人の美女があつた。幼時より、攤母の手に育てられた彼女は、世間の例に漏れなく一日として涙の乾く間とてなかつた。それは彼女が十七歳の春の一日、友達に誘はれて近くの海岸に貝拾ひに出かけたが、途中で堪へ難い臭氣の襲つて來るのを感じた。娘達は『放屁したのは誰だへ』と罵り且つ興じながら、やがて海岸に來れば最早や太陽は高く昇つてゐた。一同は潮の引くのを待つ間、携へ來つた辨當を開いた。──と彼女の辨當は外部は美しい器であつたが、その中には人糞が溢るゝばかり盛られてあつた一同はそれと見てどつと聲をあげて笑つた。

（49）

「途々臭いと思つたら、お辨當が糞だつてよ」

「妾しは、まだ糞なんか食べる光榮を有しないことよ」

「糞だつて、かまやあしない。誰だつて、お腹の中にはあるんですものホッホッ……」

娘達の嘲弄の的となつた彼女は、燃ゆる樣に赤くなつて、双の眼からは、熱い涙がホロ〳〵と零れた。無心な娘達も、流石この可憐な有樣を見ては、今更らながら氣の毒になつた。そして、今迄で此の同情心のなかつた自身を責める心は、やがて同情の涙と變つて來た。

「何んて憎らしい女だらう」

「ほんとに、邪見にも程があるわ」

「妾等みんなで、復讐してやらう……」

今迄で默つて泣いてゐた彼女は、この時夜の言葉を遣つて云つた。

「皆さん！お志ざしはありがとうよ。しかし、これはお母さんが惡いのではなくつてよ。妾さへ家にゐなければ、お母さんはきつと善い人とならるゝでしやう。さうだ、妾は今より天に昇つて、安樂に暮しませう。ねえ皆さま、五日の後に夜の月を見て、若しやその中に足を延ばして籠を傍にをき、やすらかに休んでゐる娘がゐましたなら、それが妾しだと思つて下さい。妾し、今日はこの嚴の上で、月の昇るのを待ちませう。さらば皆さん！」

娘達は、其の心中を汲みて止むる心も出です、涙ながら『さようなら〳〵』と呼びかはしながら蹈つて行つた。翌日、このことを聞き傳へた彼女の父は、狂氣の如くなつて海岸に來り尋ね廻つたが、遂に可愛い娘の姿は見えなかつた泣く泣く我が家に歸り、五日後

鷺になつた娘の話

最一つ、繼母と娘の哀れなお話しをしやう。或る日のこと、夫の獵に出かけたのを見すました繼母は、娘のカボシを呼んで水を汲み來れと命じた。カボシはおとなしく言はれるま〻に家を出たが、可弱き女の身に幾路を越ゆれど、水泉む溪とてはなかつた、俄は次第にせまるに漸くのことで我が家に歸り來つた。そして、母の前に兩手をついて願つた。

『お母さま、お腹が減つて堪へられません。どうか、一杯の御飯を下さいませ』

それを聴いた繼母は、目に角を立て〻云つた。

『お前などにやる飯は、一粒だつてありやあしない。お前の水汲みがあまりに遲いものだから、殘りの飯はみんな犬に吳れてやつたさ』

カボシは、露ほどの惜もなき繼母のさうした言葉に、娘心にワツとそこに泣き伏した。暫くして、漸く心をとりなほしたカボシは・か〻る非道の母に仕へんよりは、寧ろ鳥となつて思ふま〻空を飛翔しやうと決心した。そして、庭に出でて帶を腰に帶び、兩手に箕を持つて二三度打ち振るに不思議や可愛いカボシは忽ち鳥となつて、ヒラ〳〵と庭木の小枝にとまつた。

斯くとは知らない父は、歸り來つて娘の姿の見えないのに、妻を近くへ呼んで訊ねた。

『カボシは如何うしたのだ。俺が獵に出た後は、お前と娘の二人きりだから、お前はカ

（51）

ポシの居る處を知つてゐる筈だ』

夫の言葉に、妻は腹立たし氣に庭の樹を指さして云つた。

『ハイ、貴郎の可愛いいカボシは、鳥になつたんですよ。御覽なさい、あの木の枝にゐ
るのが、不幸者のカボシが成れの果てなんです』

思ひがけなくもたつた一人の娘が鳥となつたと聞いて父は、身も世もあらず泣き悲しみ

早速獵し得た肉を手にして其の樹の下に行き

『カボシ！カボシ！お前が好きな肉を上げる。さあ、早く元の姿となつて吳れ』

と泣きながら云つた。然し、この慈愛深き父の言葉も、あさましい鳥となつては解する

に由なかつたか、娘の鳥は羽翼もせず樹下を飛んでゐた。父はあまりの悲しさに、只茫然

と立つてゐたのであるが、不思議や其の父の首は自らポタリと落ちた。

──悲道の繼母の言葉こそ、ポタリと落ちて然るべきを、何の罪罰もなき慈父の首を落す

とは、それはたとへ鳥類になつたとは云へ、あまりに淺間しい處業ではないか。閑話休題

その娘のカボシの變じた鳥こそ、今日の世の鷺の親先である。

女人が森の話

むかし、一人の若い獵人があつた。晨の露を踏み分けて、とある森の奥深く辿り行つた

處、そこには未だ會つて見も聞きもしない蕃社があつて、その蕃社には美しい女人ばかり

が住んでゐた。そして、其の女人達がかなでる樂器の妙なる管は、靜かな林間に夢のやう

に響き渡つてそれは何んとも玄ひやうもなき神祕な世界をなしてゐた。若き獵人は、この

不思議な光景に我れを忘れて、たゞ茫然と眺め入るばかりであつた。──と、一人の女人

が他の女人に何事かさゝやくよと見れば、多くの女人達は胡蝶のやうに美しく獵人の周圍をとりかこんだ。

「モシ若い獵人さん、あなたは一體何處から來られました」

「僕は、この森の外に住んでゐる人間です。つい道を踏み迷うて、こゝまで參りました

それにしても、不可思議なるは貴女達の樣子ｰｰ」

「ホッホッ……妾達はこの森の精よ。この森は、女人が森と云つて、妾達の自由の天地よ。アラそんなに驚かれなくつてようムんす。ほんとに珍らしいお客人！ねえ皆さん、妾達はこの珍らしいお客人に御馳走を致しませう」

女人達は、無理無慙に手を執つて、若い獵人を家の中に伴ひ込んだ。そして、窓の戸といふ戸は悉く閉されたのであるが、暫くして緣側に出た獵人の顏色は靑ざめ、霬の生氣は時ならず森の沈默を破つた。

「アレ何處へ行かれたかと思へば、殿はこゝにゐられましたかえ」

「若い獵人さん、妾達はもう殿を虐めない事よ。こんどこそ、ほんとうに御馳走しませう」

「ほんと、ほんと。さあ妾達と一所に……」

口々に憑う云ひながら、女達は獵人を食堂に伴つて行つた。がしかし、不思議や女人達はたゞ湯氣を吸ふのみで、釜の中の肉や薯をつけなかつた。獵人は、或は女達は肉や薯の美味を知らないではないかと、先づ釜の中から一片の肉を取り出して食した。ｰｰと、女人達はさつと顏色を變へて互に顏を見合せたが、やがて一人の女人が聲も荒々しく

て（53）

云つた。

「殿の獵人とは僞りでしやう。此の森の外の人間とは眞赤な嘘でしやう」

この意外な言葉に、獵人は箸を投げて答へた。

「イヤ僕は僞りは云はない、人間に相違ありません」

「白々しく申さるな、姿達は湯氣と空氣とのみ吸つて生きてゐるのに、同じ人間と云は
る〻殿が、どうして肉を召し上つた。肉を食ふのは豚よ。粟を食ふのは豚
！豚とは知らず擥せし惜けなさ、今までの愛が一時に憎しみとなつて、獵人を檻の中に投げ込んで了
つた。斯くて其の日の夜は來たけれど、女人達は一人としてそこに近づく者とてなかつた
獵人は何事も運命であると沈默をつゞけてゐたが、ふと耳を澄せば何處よりか徹かに唄の
聲が聞へて來た。

妹脊の間、つゆ僞りがあらうぞ
私の峠は活きてゐる。

若し僞りあらば
私の手には太刀がある⋯⋯⋯⋯⋯。
その妙なる唄の主は誰ぞ、恰もる月光にすかし見れば、そこには一人の美しい女が立つ
てゐた。

「若し旅の獵人さん、こゝにゐらしてはお命が危ふムいます。寸時も早くお逃げ下さい
ませ」

「あ〻貴女は⋯⋯⋯⋯」

「シッ！お聲が高い」

「貴女は、僕が多くの女人達に虐れてゐた時、遠くの木影に一人淋しさうに立つてゐた方！さうだ、さうしてその清い目に露を宿してゐた方！その貴女が、如何して此處に來られました」

「妾しは元とからこの森の女人ではムいません。ふと道を踏み迷つてこの森に入り、遂に森の女人の召使ひとして今日まで暮してゐるのでムいます……」

「お～それでは貴女はやつぱり僕と同じ人間！あ～僕と同じ人間！」

「妾し、殿のお姿を見て故郷の父母が戀しくなりました……」

「尤もです。さあそれでは僕と一所に、此處から逃げ出しませう……」

「イエ、妾しは頭底逃れることは出來ません。何事も運命と覺悟しております。アレアレ家の中の女人達が目醒めたやうです。妾しに闘つてゐては、お命が危ふムいます。さあ早くお逃げ下さいませ」

「有難う、貴女の御恩は死すとも忘れは致しません」

「何んの御禮に及びましやうぞ、これもみんな森の女人達の惡戲からでムいます。さあこの柵の隙間から早く～～」

獵人は「さらば」と一目散に駈け出したが、心ひかる～ま～ふと後を振り向けば、そこには夜の目にもくつきりと白う彼女の顏が闇の中に浮いてゐた……。

（41）

傳說の高砂族（五）

秋澤烏川

穿山甲ご猿の話

猿智惠——といふ言葉がある。猿は昔から小智惠の所有者といふことに相場が定つてゐる。ある山里に、穿山甲と猿が棲んでゐた。一日釣竿を肩に、近くの河に魚釣りに行つたが、その日は大漁で大きい籠に一杯の獲物を得、喜び勇んで我家に歸つて來た。ところが、穿山甲は喉が渴いて致方なく、猿に水を汲んで來る樣に命じた。猿は早速心得た樣をして家を出たが、暫くすると竹の水筒を持つて歸り來つた。穿山甲は、今その竹筒を受け取つて一口飮うとしたが、プンと臭氣が鼻を衝いた。

『オイ君！これは小便ではないか』

『馬鹿を云ひ玉ふな、僕は小便など汲んだ覺へはない。たしかに、泉の水なんだ。如何して君にはそんなに臭いだらう。若しや君は、自身で小便を乘れてゐるではないかね。兎角腹が冷たくなると、小便が出ても覺へないものだが……』

『オイ君は何處までも、人を嘲弄するんだナ。論より證據だ、この惡臭を嗅げ！』

白々しい猿の言葉にたまりかねた穿山甲は、怒う云つて其の竹筒を猿の鼻先きに突きつけたが、猿はそれに相手にならなかつた。穿山甲は致方なく、自分でノコ〳〵と水を汲みに出て行つた。その後姿を見送つた猿は、ニタリと笑つて『人は欺き易いものだわい』と

（42）

獨り言を云ひながら、籠の中の魚を一人で喰つて了つた。かくて穿山甲の矢の鏃の先きを
聞くして、素知らぬ顔で澄し込んでゐた。そして、歸り來つた穿山甲に云つた。

『君！今君の留守に大きい鳥が一羽飛んで來て、魚をみんな食つて了つた。僕は腹だ〜し
さに、其の鳥を一矢に射止めんとしたが、不思議やその矢は鳥には立たず。嶺がこんなに
聞くなつちやつた』

カンニングな猿が試かしの言葉を聽き終つた穿山甲は、何んと思つたのか一つの杖を持
ち來つて身も輕ろく屋根の上に飛びあがり、また地上に飛びおりなどして見せた。猿の人
眞假、負け嫌ひの猿は謀られたとは知らず。早速その杖を執つて同じく飛び上り飛び下り
したが、何が裂て腹一杯の魚は、糞尿と共に一時にどつと出た。この羅擺を握られては、流
石の厚顔の猿も一言の抗靜もなく恐れ入つてしまつた。ある日、二人は山に行つて茅を燒いたが、腹に一物ある穿山
甲は兼々として燃へつ〜ある彼方を指さして云つた。

『誰か彼の火中に入る者ぞ、君は生來の怯懦者だから、火を見るさへ恐うしいだらう』
怯懦者と云はれて負け嫌いの猿は、身を震はして憤慨した。

『君に出來ることなら、僕には朝飯前のことだ』
穿山甲はこの猿の音叢を聽くと、茅の中に躍り込み、猿の放つ火に包まれてしまつた。
やがて、火の消えると共に平氣な顔をして燒け跡から出て來た。

『オイ君は、どうして燒けないのだ』
穿山甲が地中深く潜んでゐたと知らない猿は、不可思議に思つて怪う聞いた。

『乾いた茅を身に覆つてゐた迄さ』

（43）

この穿山甲の言葉を信じてそれを眞似た猿が、やがて黑燒となつて現れたのは云ふ迄でもない。穿山甲はその燒死した猿の腹を割いて肉を取り去り、再び元のやうに縫ひ合して呪文を唱へてゐたが、不可思議や猿は蘇生した。ふと氣づいた猿は、自分の腹が馬鹿にからつぽになつてゐるので、傍に落ちてゐる肉を甘まさうに喰つた。それを見た穿山甲は『己の肉を喰ふ奴人！』と罵りながら、土の中にもぐつて了つた。猿は致方なくこんどは河岸に來つて釣を垂れたが、その日はどうしたものか一尾の魚も釣れなかつた。茫然と水の上を凝視してゐると、目の眞黑い大きい怪物が現れたので、猿は命からぐ逃げ跡つた。

と、家には穿山甲がニコ／＼して待つてゐた。

「ハッ……オイ、何んでそんなに狼狽してゐるんだ」

「イヤ君、實際驚いたよ。何しろ僕は今日まであんな化物を見たことがない」

「ハァあの河の怪物か、あれは君があまり性質が惡いので、犬方水神が怒られたんだらう。もう河に行くのは止めて、これから二人で山へ木の實を探りに行かう」

「有難い、やつぱり持つべきは知己だ」

其の翌日二人は打ち連れて山に行つた。そこには大きい樹に赤い實が累々として熟れてわた。猿はスル／＼と幹から枝に登つて、甘味さうな奴を獨りでムシャ／＼と頰張つた。

「オイ君！僕にも一つ吳れ玉へ」

「オヤ君は家へ歸つたと思つたら、まだそこにゐたのかへ。待ち玉へ、甘いのをやるよ」

猿は自分の股の肉に挿んでゐた實を下に投げた。それとは知らない穿山甲は、喜びながら拾ひ取るが早いか一目に喰つたが、覆郁たらざる臭氣はブーンと鼻を衝いた。それを樹

の上で見てゐた猿は、大聲をあげてカラ／＼と笑つた。――朱襄の仁とは、蓋しこの穿山甲の謂であらう。

刺青の始つた話

太古、山も野も鬱蒼たる樹木生ひ茂り、累々たる木の實四季を絶えず熟する平和の世界に、唯一人の美女が住んでゐた。晨に緑蔭に唄ひ、夕べに千草を敷きて伏床としてゐたが、一日春風を孕んで月滿ち、玉のやうな男の子を生み落した。

『何んといふ小さい可愛い子だらう……』

自分より他に人間を見たことのなかつた彼女は、怨う云つて頬ずりをしながら、美しい木の實を與へなどした。――月日の立つは早瀬の如く、それから二十年の歳華は夢の樣に流れた。若々しかつた彼女も、最早や三十五歳の母親となり、小さい赤ん坊だつた子は、二十歳の男盛りとなつた。或る日のこと、母親の仕事をしてゐる姿をつく／＼見守つてゐた息子は、何を思ひ出したのか母に言葉をかけた。

『お母さん！お母さんは僕一人で淋しくはありませんか。僕ね、此頃なんだかお母さんと二人ぎりでは淋しくてなりません』

母親は、息子の顔をジロリと見やつたが、暫くして云つた。

『お前は、何んといふ小心者だらう。お母さんは女の身でありながら、生れて十五年といふものは一人で暮し、それからお前を産んでから更に二十年にもなるが、たつた一度だつて淋しいなんかと思つたことがない。それにお前は男のくせに何んといふ小心者だらう……

…………。

〈45〉

『デモお母さん、僕はこの頃毎夜夢を見るのよ』

『夢！夢！』

『アラお母さんも夢を見る？僕ね、毎夜それは！〜美しい樂しい夢を見るのよ』

『夢！夢!!その夢は……』

母親の勢込んだ間に、息子はほんのり顔を赤めて云つた。

『それは、お母さんの前だつて云へやしない美しい樂しい夢よ。僕ね、その夢から醒める

と、淋しくて淋しくて致方がないのです』

彼女は、その上はもう聽かうとはしなかつた。自分は、何んといふ情知らずの人間であ

つたらう。自分が自然に生れたのだから、惣の思ひやりとてもなかつたが、息子は自分の

腹から生れた者だ。年頃ともなれば、戀の心も萠生えやう。さうだ、自分は息子の嫁を探さ

ねばならない………。かう決心した彼女は、其の翌日から毎日！〜野の草を分け、山の

惆々の間をくまなく探ね求めたが一人の女とても見出すことが出來なかつた。がつかりした

彼女は、とある岩の上に腰を掛けて何事か考へてゐたが、聽てハタと膝を打つて立ち上つ

た。

『この上は、自分が姿を變へて息子の嫁になる外はない』

其の日は、何時になく晴々しい心持ちで我家に歸つて來た。そして、息子に云つた。

『今日お母さんは、お前にいゝ嫁さんを探して來ました。で、明朝あの谷向ひの岩の上に

お出で、そこにはきつと、お前と同じ樣に淋しい思ひを胸に抱いてゐる美しい花嫁がお前

を待つてゐるでしやう。このお母さんは、お前に嫁を貰へば用のない身なんですから、こ

れより幾酢越へた遠い處へ行きます。二人は、何時までも！〜も仲よく暮すのですよ』

（46）

母親は悵う立つたまゝ、やがて家を出て行つた。息子は不思議な思ひをして、翌朝母に
敎へられた通り谷の向ひに行つた處、そこには顔を黒く染めた（刺青）美しい女が正裝して
待つてゐた。

『おゝ貴郎は妾の夫！』
『おゝ貴女は我が妻！』

二人が固く握る手は、永遠に變らぬ夫婦の契りとはなつた。　乃ち母親なる彼女は、
我が息子を僞るために己の顔に刺青をしたのである。星霜邁る幾百年、今日に至るまでそ
の子孫である高砂族の婦が、夫を持つ時は必らず顔に刺青をする風習は、この物語に起因
すると傳へられてゐる。

無人島の話

漸くのことで、とある孤島の巖陰に漂い著いた兄妹の二人は、海水にぬれた衣の袖を互
に絞りながら、今のあたりに見た恐ろしい光景を靜かに囘想した。――――山嶽の轟然と
して崩るゝよと見れば、火燄天に沖して日月ために光りなく、人畜の悲鳴の山河の震動の
響と合して凄然たる濁水はやがて夫等の總てを呑み去つた。……沈著
なる二人の兄妹は、その激動のなかにあて素早くも一本の樹を伐り倒して丸木舟を造り、
それに打ち乘つては波のまにくに漂ひながら、流れ寄る繁の穂を拾ひつゝその生死を天
運に委せてゐたのであるが、不思議にも萬死に一生を得て夕せまる頃、この小島に漂ひ著
いたのであつた。さうして二人は神の冥加をうち悦びて、ほつと安き息を吐いた。

『兄さん、こゝは如何した島？』

（47）

妹に聲をかけられてはじめて我に返つた兄は、四方をジロ〱見廻してゐたが、そこに
は家しらものとてもなく、自分等の外には人影も見えなかつた。

『さうだ、怎うして目に觸る〱何物もないのを見ると、こゝは無人島かも知れない』

『無人島！無人島‼』

『さうだ、きつと無人島であらう。イヤ妹よ、何もさう泣くことはない。あの恐ろしい世
界から遁れてこの島に漂ひ來つたのも、やつぱり神の恩加といふものだ。もう日はとつぷ
りと暮れて四方は暗くなつた。今夜はこの荒磯で假寢しやうに

二人の兄妹は、互に手を握り合つて冷たき夢を結んだ。目醒むれば、キラ〱として眩し
いほどの太陽が高く昇つてゐた。二人は若しや人は住んでゐないかと、此方彼を探ね步
いたけれど、遂にそれはみんな徒勞であつた。斯くと知つた兄は妹を勵まして小屋を造り、
田圃を開いて襲に食ひ殘した一穗の粟を蒔き、こゝにさゝやかなる生活を營むこと〱なつ
た。それから日を送り月を迎ふる幾十回、四顧茫渺たる孤島の心さびしさは、唯に妹一人
のみではなかつた。ある夜のこと、兄は妹に向つて云つた。

『妹よ、我等は何んといふ不幸者であらう。父母を亡つて間もなきに、彼の悲慘なる歷史
の舟に送られてこの島に漂ひ著いたのであるが、將來を思ひ考ふれば、この侘寂しき孤島
の生活は、二人の生活にとつて決して幸福ではない。二人年老ひ果て〱手足の不自由を感
ずるに至らば・誰が我等を養ひ吳れるのだ。妹よ、決して驚いてはならない。我が言は未だ世に偶なきことではある
が、我等二人夫婦となりてその幸福と繁榮を計るのが、我等を救ひ玉ひし神に對する道だ
と思ふ、イヤさう確信する……』

また病みて斃すれば、何人が亡き我等の靈を
弔ひ吳れるのだ。

意外なること兄の言葉に、妹は顔を米のやうに赫めて身動きもしなかつた。……二人の間には、暫らく沈黙がつゞいた。皎々たる月はいつしか雲間にかくれて、孤島の夜は深く波の背に更けて行つた。――歳華流水と去つてそれから十数年を經る時には、最早や二人の中には十数人の子女を有してゐた。にそこに一の部落を成した。一日、鍛冶を業とせる兄の子女も互に夫婦となり、寵を分つて逢したものかその目は鐵が火の粉となつて四散して臼から飛び出して了つた。農を業としてゐる兄妹の一組が粟飯を搗いてゐたが、これも亦辭けて家財鐵類器額を舟に積み、父母兄妹に別れを告げた。妹は、鰭の身に迫るを恐れて

「お父さん、お母さん、兄妹の哲さん、惡魔に呪はれた私共は、彼の雲の果てなる遠い國に行きます。思へば幾年月住み馴れしこの島も、今が見納めでムいます。だが私共は彼の來兒の國に赴し、そこにまた新らしい村を拓くでありませう。そこには、御兩親の温い血を享けた私共兄妹の人々が、生の喜びを壓謝するでせう。さらば……」と、南颶に帆は高く張られ、軈て船は懐しい故郷の島を後に、浪路遙に消えて行つた。島に殘りしは高砂族の龍先で、島を出でしは臺灣人の祖先である。されぱこそ今日我等高砂族には鐵が勘く、彼等臺灣人には鐵が多いのに不思議はあるまい……と、老頭目は語り終つて盃を手にした。

祭の夜の話

むかし、或る山里にサツーと呼ぶ極めて美しい少女があつた。一日母のブゴウに伴はれ、兄のアリモローと共に山畑に草刈りに行つた。庭が、……と、可弱き乙女のサツーは、疲れ果てゝ氣も心もなく何時しか一本の木蔭に深き眠りについた。時は、身はいつしか未だ見も聞きもしたことのない大きい家の中に寝かされてゐた。彼等女はたゞボンヤリと夢見心地に周圍を物奇らしげに眺めてゐたが、そこにノソリ／＼と一人

（49）

の頭目が現れて來るのであつた。

「少女よ、お前は今日からこゝの家族となるのだよ。いゝか、この俺の娘となるのだよ」

それと聽いたサツーは、怖れ戰きシクゝと泣き出した。

「少女よ、何もさう泣くことはないではないか。あの小ぼけな家の娘より、この頭目の娘となるのがいくらいゝか知れない。お前は、ほんとに幸福者である」

この時、サツーは始めて口を開いた。

「若し頭目さん、私はどうして茲に來たんでしやう」

そのサツーの言葉を聽いた頭目は、今迄での優しさと打つて變つて聲も荒々しく、怒氣滿面に朱をそゝいで怒號した。

「そんなことを、汝が聞く必要はない。イヤサ、聞きたければ聞かしてやる。俺は、汝が彼の木蔭に眠つてゐる庭をそのまゝ抱いて歸つたのだ。汝がさうしたことも知らず、俺の腕に熟睡して懲炭を浮べてゐるに反し、汝の母と兄は狂氣の如くなつて騷いでゐたのさ八ツハツ……」

かうなれば、サツーは最早やどうする事も出來なかつた。唯自身の運命を天に委すより外衞とてもなかつた。——月日は流水に似て春を送り秋を迎へる事數回に及んだ。サツーは今日では花も恥ぢらう十八歳となつたある夏の夜のことであつた。突然一人の靑年が彼女の家を訪ねて來た。サツーはその地の風習として、水を汲みてその客人の前に出でた。と靑年はまたゝきもせず彼女の顏を見てゐたが、やがて靜に言葉をかけた。

「甚だ失禮ですが、貴女のお名は何んと云はれます」

花ならば將に綻びん妙齢のサツーは、慈う若者から聲をかけられてはんのりと顏に紅葉を散らした。

「妾、サツーと申します」

「サツー！サツー！」

（50）

『アレぞ姿の名をお聞きになすつてそんなに驚かれるのは……』

『お前こそは幾年かけて尋ぬる我が妹だ』

『えッ！それでは貴郎は兄さん！あゝお逢ひしたかつた。姿し……』

サツーは『姿し』とまで云つたが、あまりの嬉しさにそれから言葉もつゞかなかつた。

『サツー、もう何も心配することはない。私には、いゝ謀計がある』

兄のアリモローが妹の耳に何事かさゝやくかと見れば、妹のサツーは泪もつ目に涼しい笑を湛へた。その事あつて数日を經た或る夜、其の社に於て盛大なる祭りが催された。社中の若者達は一人も殘らや出でゝ強い酒を酌み、その中央に美しい祭物サツーを立たせて踊り狂つた。……と、此時背後の劇竹颪もなきに揺るると見れば、その先端に一人の美服を著けた若者が現れ、竹の曲ると共に人々の中央に降り來つたが、素早くも彼の美女を小脇に抱へてそのまゝ再び空中高く跳ね上つて間に姿を消して了つた。若者達の歓興の中心であつた美女サツーを奪はれた一同は、夢から醒めたやうにケロリとした顔を互に見合した。

『君！いま空中から美しい著物を著て降りて來たのは何んだね』

『僕には皆目辨明んなァ』

『あのサツーを抱いて其の儘再び空中高く跳び上つた早業は、とても人間の業ではないよ』。

『さうだ、あれはきつと神様なんだ』

ここで酒宴は撤せられ、代るに嚴かなる祭壇は設けられた。そして、人々は其の前に跪いて祈りをあげた。空には金剛石を散らしたかのやうにキラ／＼星が輝いて、蕃社の夜は静に深く更けて行くのであつた。……。

怨うした物語を探ねて行けば、まだいくらもありますけれど、あまり長くなつては讀者諸君の御迷惑と思ひますので、一先づこれを以て『傳説の高砂族』は終りと致します。そして明けて茅出度き新春より、更に罪現を改めて何か書こうと思つてゐます。

作者	原文	譯文	出處
秋澤烏川	傳說の高砂族（一）	傳說的高砂族（一）	《臺灣警察協會雜誌》87，1924.8.25
秋澤烏川	傳說の高砂族（二）	傳說的高砂族（二）	《臺灣警察協會雜誌》88，1924.9.25
秋澤烏川	傳說の高砂族（三）	傳說的高砂族（三）	《臺灣警察協會雜誌》89，1924.10.25
秋澤烏川	傳說の高砂族（四）	傳說的高砂族（四）	《臺灣警察協會雜誌》90，1924.11.25
秋澤烏川	傳說の高砂族（五）	傳說的高砂族（五）	《臺灣警察協會雜誌》91，1924.12.25

出處一覽表

附錄二　參與者簡介

附錄二　參與者簡介

作者

秋澤烏川

　　本名秋澤次郎，日本高知縣出身。曾任職於總督府的諸多單位，如臺南地方法院、法務部民刑課、警務局警務課、總督官房法務課等。同時也在《臺法月報》、《臺灣警察協會雜誌》擔任編輯。一九二六年一月返回日本內地，成為《大阪朝日新聞》記者，之後曾數次從大阪將短歌創作投稿至《臺灣日日新報》。著有《臺灣名流卓上一夕話》、《臺灣匪誌》，亦曾編輯《臺灣總督府警察職員錄》、《臺灣總督府警察法規》等。

主編

許俊雅

　　現任臺灣師範大學國文學系特聘教授兼系主任。著有《日據時期臺灣小說研究》、《臺灣文學論——從現代到當代》、《島嶼容顏——臺灣文學評論集》、《見樹又見林——文學看臺灣》、《瀛海探珠——走向臺灣古典文學》、《裨海紀遊校釋》、《梁啟超林獻堂往來書札編注》、《足音集》、《低眉集》等，編有《全臺賦》、《全臺詞》（合編）、《王昶雄全集》、《黎烈文全集》、《中國現代文學選》、《日治時期臺灣小說選讀》、《臺灣小說·青春讀本》、《巫永福精選集》、《臺灣日治時期翻譯文學作品集》等。

中譯

鳳氣至純平，日本橫濱人。成功大學臺灣文學系博士。現任文藻外語大學日本語文系兼任助理教授。譯有《同化的同床異夢：日治時期臺灣的語言政策、近代化與認同》、《神國日本荒謬的決戰生活》。

許倍榕，臺南人。成功大學臺灣文學系博士。曾執筆《望鄉：父親郭雪湖的藝術生涯》，譯有《神國日本荒謬的決戰生活》。

英譯

崔麿，現就讀英國杜倫大學博士班，由政治思想史的角度研究保守主義的流派與變遷。譯有《思考：哲學裡的星星、月亮、太陽》（合譯）。

插圖

分輯插圖／汪凱彬，國立臺灣師範大學美術學系博士生。喜愛原住民族，曾從事相關文化工作，感佩原住民族尊重自然、生命與天地的觀念和傳統，也對於過去原住民的生活模式與居住領域、其留下珍貴之文化資產及族群智慧有著濃厚的興趣。

內頁插圖／陳映蹀，臺北人，一九九〇年生，輔仁大學中國文學系畢業。曾任第十四屆新店高級中學漫畫研究社社長，前職為網路遊戲公司 3D 美術人員，現階段為自由接案設計者。常用軟體為 Photoshop，偏好半寫實與漫畫式的繪圖風格，喜歡將文字敘述或想法化為圖畫的過程，並將其實踐為作品。

文學研究叢書·臺灣文學叢刊 0810010

傳說的高砂族

作　　　者	秋澤烏川
主　　　編	許俊雅
中　　　譯	鳳氣至純平、許倍榕
英　　　譯	崔　麿
繪　　　者	汪凱彬、陳映蹀
責任編輯	廖宜家
特約校稿	林秋芬

發 行 人	陳滿銘
總 經 理	梁錦興
總 編 輯	陳滿銘
副總編輯	張晏瑞
編 輯 所	萬卷樓圖書股份有限公司
排　　版	林曉敏
印　　刷	維中科技有限公司
封面設計	菩薩蠻數位文化有限公司

發　　行　萬卷樓圖書股份有限公司
　　　　　臺北市羅斯福路二段 41 號 6 樓之 3
　　　　　電話 (02)23216565
　　　　　傳真 (02)23218698
　　　　　電郵 SERVICE@WANJUAN.COM.TW
香港經銷　香港聯合書刊物流有限公司
　　　　　電話 (852)21502100
　　　　　傳真 (852)23560735

ISBN 978-986-478-220-8
2018 年 11 月初版一刷
定價：新臺幣 280 元

如何購買本書：

1. 劃撥購書，請透過以下郵政劃撥帳號：
　　帳號：15624015
　　戶名：萬卷樓圖書股份有限公司
2. 轉帳購書，請透過以下帳戶
　　合作金庫銀行　古亭分行
　　戶名：萬卷樓圖書股份有限公司
　　帳號：0877717092596
3. 網路購書，請透過萬卷樓網站
　　網址 WWW.WANJUAN.COM.TW

大量購書，請直接聯繫我們，將有專人為
您服務。客服：(02)23216565　分機 610

如有缺頁、破損或裝訂錯誤，請寄回更換

國家圖書館出版品預行編目資料

傳說的高砂族 / 秋澤烏川著；許俊雅編.--
初版.-- 臺北市　：萬卷樓, 2018.11
面 ；　公分. -- (文學研究叢書 ；0810010)

ISBN 978-986-478-220-8(平裝)

539.5339　　　　　　　　107016864